face2face

Pre-intermediate Workbook

400

Nicholas Tims with Chris Redston & Gillie Cunningham

CAMBRIDGE UNIVERSITY PRESS
Cambridge, New York, Melbourne, Madrid, Cape Town, Singapore, São Paulo

Cambridge University Press
The Edinburgh Building, Cambridge CB1 2RU, UK

www.cambridge.org
Information on this title: www.cambridge.org/9780521613972

First published 2005
Reprinted 2005

Printed in Italy by Legoprint S.p.A.

A catalogue record for this publication is available from the British Library

ISBN-13   978-0-521-613972 Workbook with Key
ISBN-10   0-521-61397-3 Workbook with Key

ISBN-13   978-0-521-60335-5 Student's Book with CD-ROM/Audio CD
ISBN-10   0-521-60335-8 Student's Book with CD-ROM/Audio CD

ISBN-13   978-0-521-61396-5 Teacher's Book
ISBN-10   0-521-61396-5 Teacher's Book

ISBN-13   978-0-521-60339-3 Class Audio CDs
ISBN-10   0-521-60339-0 Class Audio CDs

ISBN-13   978-0-521-60343-0 Class Audio Cassettes
ISBN-10   0-521-60343-9 Class Audio Cassettes

ISBN-13   978-0-521-61399-6 Network CD-ROM
ISBN-10   0-521-61399-X Network CD-ROM

ISBN-13   978-8-483-23371-9 Student's Book with CD-ROM/Audio CD, Spanish edition
ISBN-10   8-483-23371-1 Student's Book with CD-ROM/Audio CD, Spanish edition

ISBN-13   978-3-12-539737-8 Student's Book with CD-ROM/Audio CD, Klett edition
ISBN-10   3-12-539737-5 Student's Book with CD-ROM/Audio CD, Klett edition

| V | Vocabulary | G | Grammar | RW | Real World | R | Reading | W | Writing |

Contents

1 Work, rest and play
Language Summary 1, Student's Book p119

1A Life stories

Question words V1.1

1 Fill in the gaps with the correct question words. Then match questions 1–8 to answers a)–h).

1 *What* languages do you speak? *f)*

2 .... does Jamie Oliver come from? ....

3 .... has the most interesting job you know? ....

4 .... did she get married? ....

5 .... are you studying English? ....

6 .... is a university degree course in England? ....

7 .... brothers and sisters have you got? ....

8 .... do you go to the cinema? ....

a) Three or four years.
b) Every weekend. I love films.
c) My brother – he's a musician in a band.
d) Essex in England.
e) About three years ago – it was a lovely wedding.
f) French and a little Spanish.
g) I want to get a better job.
h) One brother and one sister.

Review of verb forms and questions G1.1

2 Fill in the gaps with *do*, *did* or *are*.

1 Who *do* you live with? My family.

2 When .... you get married? Last May.

3 What .... you going to do tonight? Watch TV.

4 Why .... you studying English? For work.

5 Where .... you going on holiday this year? To the beach.

6 How many countries .... you visit last year? Lots.

7 What .... you doing at the moment? I'm studying English.

8 What .... you do in your free time? Go shopping.

3 a) Read the interviews and write a question from **2** in the correct places A–D.

Do you have an interesting life?
We asked four people four questions.
Do they have interesting lives? You decide.

A *What are you doing at the moment?*

SAM   I'm going to a meeting. I work for a TV company. We ¹ *'re doing* (do) a series with a famous chef at the moment.

ANNIE   It's my brother's birthday tomorrow. So I ² .... (look) for a present.

BOB   We're going to the cinema. We often go on Fridays.

Sam

B ....

SAM   Free time? Work is the best free time activity!

ANNIE   Well, I've got three children so I ³ .... (not have got) much free time. I love skiing. We went skiing in Italy last year.

HEIDI   Well, we like films. Sometimes we get a DVD. And Bob ⁴ .... (play) the guitar.

Annie

C ....

SAM   Italy, Spain, the USA and Brazil. All for work, of course.

ANNIE   Well, I ⁵ .... (tell) you about skiing in Italy. We also stayed with friends in Scotland. Next year we're going to visit Spain.

BOB   We spent two weeks in Wales on a camping holiday. It rained most of the time, but we ⁶ .... (go) for some nice walks.

Bob and Heidi

D ....

SAM   Well, this meeting is going to finish late. Then I ⁷ .... (make) some phone calls and go to a restaurant. I never eat at home.

ANNIE   My husband and I ⁸ .... (do) our homework. We're studying Spanish at the moment.

HEIDI   We want to watch a programme on TV tonight.

b) Read the interviews again and put the verbs in brackets in the Present Simple, Present Continuous, Past Simple or use *be going to*.

4 **a)** Make questions with these words.

1 is / doing / Sam / at / What / the / moment ?

   What is Sam doing at the moment?

2 did / holiday / last / go / Annie / on / year / Where ?

   ....

3 birthday / is / Annie's / brother's / When ?

   ....

4 his / What / in / does / Sam / do / free time ?

   ....

5 go / do / Heidi and Bob / cinema / When / to / the ?

   ....

6 to / Annie / this / What / going / do / is / evening ?

   ....

7 did / How / last / many / visit / countries / Sam / year ?

   ....

8 Where / on / is / holiday / next / Annie / year / going ?

   ....

9 are / What / this / do / going / to / evening / Heidi and Bob ?

   ....

10 going / Heidi and Bob / Where / are / now ?

   ....

b) Read the article in **3a)** again. Answer the questions in **4a)**.

1 *He's going to a meeting.*

2 ....
   ....

3 ....

4 ....
   ....

5 ....

6 ....
   ....

7 ....

8 ....

9 ....
   ....

10 ....
   ....

1B Super commuters

Work V1.2

1 Fill in the gaps with these words and *in*, *for*, *as* or *with*.

| a restaurant   a department store   a journalist   London   a receptionist |
| young children   unemployed people   a newspaper   teenagers   herself |

1 Ryan is a chef. He works *in a restaurant.*

2 Sally doesn't have a boss. She works ....

3 Stewart works .... He loves working in a big city.

4 Ruth works .... She helps them to find jobs.

5 Jess and Drew are teachers. They work .... and ....

6 Michael works .... called *Harrods*. The shop sells everything.

7 Lynne works .... She meets people and answers the phones.

8 Judy works .... called *The Daily Times*. She works ....

Stewart

Ruth

Michael

Judy

Subject questions G1.2

2 a) Choose the correct words.

1 Who *does work/works* as a receptionist?
2 Which newspaper *does Judy work/works Judy* for?
3 What *do Jess and Drew do/do Jess and Drew*?
4 Whose job *does help/helps* unemployed people?
5 Who *does work/works* in a kitchen?
6 Which person *does work/works* in a shop?
7 Who *hasn't got/hasn't* a boss?
8 Who *does like/likes* working in a big city?

b) Answer the questions in **2a)**.

1 _Lynne_
2
3
4
5
6
7
8

3 Look at the words in **bold**. Write two questions for each sentence. Use the Present Simple.

1 **Stewart** leaves home **at 6.30 a.m**.
  Who leaves home at 6.30 a.m?
  When does Stewart leave home?

2 **Michael** walks to work **every morning**.
  Who _____?
  How often _____?

3 **This train** goes to **London**.
  Which _____?
  Where _____?

4 **Jane** spends **£200** a week on travel.
  Who _____?
  How much _____?

4 Complete the questions in these conversations.

1 A The traffic was really bad.
  B Sorry. What _was really bad?_
  A The traffic.

2 A Ryan missed the train.
  B Sorry. Who _____?
  A Ryan.

3 A Ruth commutes to Cowley five days a week.
  B Sorry. Where _____ to?
  A Cowley, near Oxford.

4 A That book belongs to Jess.
  B Sorry. Which _____?
  A That one.

5 A Judy is waiting to see you.
  B Sorry. Who _____?
  A Judy. The journalist from *The Daily Times*.

5 Read the conversation. Write questions in the Present Simple.

Mike and Ruby Carson live in London. We asked them about their journeys to work.

Q Why / you / live in London? [1] _Why do you live in London?_

MIKE Well, I work in Cambridge and Ruby works in Oxford, so London is the best place for us to live.

Q Who / have / the longest journey? [2] _____

RUBY Mike does. I get the train and it takes about an hour. Mike gets a bus, then the tube and then the train.

Q Who / get up / first? [3] _____

MIKE Ruby does. She needs to be at work very early.

Q What / you / do, Ruby? [4] _____

RUBY I'm a doctor.

Q Who / spend / the most on travel? [5] _____

MIKE I do. I spend about £2,000 a year.

Q / you / want to get jobs in London? [6] _____

RUBY Yes, we do! I want to work at a London hospital. But at the moment, it's impossible.

Q Who / get / home first? [7] _____

MIKE I do usually and then I cook dinner!

VOCABULARY AND READING

Free time activities with *do, play, go, go to* **V1.3**

1 **a)** [S] Look at the pictures and find the words in the puzzle.

```
A  B  A  S  K  E  G  U  E  L  C  I
C  R  J  O  G  N  G  J  L  N  A  C
Y  S  T  C  I  S  O  A  M  E  R  C
O  I  E  G  R  L  B  A  U  G  B  Y
Y  L  G  Y  A  T  S  S  S  A  C
C  O  L  O  E  L  M  M  C  G  S  L
J  R  G  K  N  U  L  I  C  C  K  I
U  R  S  A  E  N  B  E  R  A  E  N
B  A  C  S  R  O  E  G  R  R  G  G
B  G  U  A  R  A  E  R  O  I  N  C
A  M  R  E  C  M  U  S  E  Y  E  R
M  C  A  R  D  S  C  Y  C  L  I  S
```

b) Complete the table with the words from **1a)**.

go	jogging
go to	
do	
play	

Frequency adverbs and expressions **V1.4**

2 Put the frequency adverbs in the correct places in these sentences.

    usually   *often*

1 I ⁄ get to the station on time, but the train is ⁄ late. (usually, often)

2 James and Maria are at home on Saturday evenings. They go to the theatre. (hardly ever, normally)

3 Are you happy? You stop smiling. (always, never)

4 Do you do any exercise? I go running. (ever, occasionally)

3 **a)** Complete the frequency expressions.

1 2/week *twice* a week

2 1/year .... a year

3 2/day .... a day

4 2–3/month .... or .... times a ....

5 1/3 months .... every .... months

6 1/day .... day

b) Look at the table and write sentences with frequency adverbs and expressions.

activity	Theo	Lily and Lionel
cook at home	a) –	f) 5–6/week
use the Internet	b) 7/week	g) –
read a newspaper	c) 1/month	h) 1/week
go the gym	d) 2–3/year	i) 3–4/month
go on holiday	e) 1/year	j) 2–3/year

a) *Theo never cooks at home.*

b) ....

c) ....

d) ....

e) ....

f) *Lily and Lionel cook at home five or six times a week.*

g) ....

h) ....

i) ....

j) ....

1D Speed dating

Finding things in common RW1.1

1 Bernie is on a speed-dating evening. Read the conversations and choose the correct words.

Clare

Isabel

Fiona

Hayley

Bernie

HAYLEY Hi. My name's Hayley. I'm a bit nervous!

BERNIE Don't worry! [1](So am I.)/Neither am I. I'm Bernie.

HAYLEY So, what do you do, Bernie?

BERNIE I work for myself.

HAYLEY Really? [2]So do I!/Neither do I!

ISABEL I eat out a lot. I don't have time to cook at home.

BERNIE [3]Oh, I don't./Neither do I. What's your favourite food?

ISABEL I love Italian food.

BERNIE [4]So am I!/Me too! I eat a lot of pasta.

CLARE I went speed dating last week, too.

BERNIE [5]So am I!/So did I! Did you meet anyone interesting?

CLARE No, I didn't like anyone!

BERNIE [6]Me neither./So did I. But it was fun!

CLARE Yes, it was.

FIONA Well, I love exercise. I go jogging every day.

BERNIE [7]Oh, I don't./Neither do I. Do you do any other sports?

FIONA No. I can't play football or tennis.

BERNIE [8]Neither can I./I can't. But I try!

2 Look at what Bernie, Isabel and Hayley said on their speed-dating evening. Then complete conversations 1–8 with the correct phrases. Sometimes there is more than one answer.

	Bernie	Isabel	Hayley
drives	✗	✗	–
has got a cat	✓	–	✓
is a vegetarian	✗	✗	–
went on holiday last year	✓	–	✗
can speak Italian	✗	✓	–
has got his/her own flat	✗	✗	–
hates working at weekends	✓	–	✓
is hot	✓	–	✓

1

BERNIE I don't drive.

ISABEL *Neither do I.* I prefer public transport.

2

BERNIE I've got a cat.

HAYLEY ....! What's yours called?

3

ISABEL I'm not a vegetarian.

BERNIE ...., but I don't eat a lot of meat.

4

HAYLEY I didn't go on holiday last year.

BERNIE .... I went to Australia. My brother lives there.

5

BERNIE I love Italian food, but I can't speak the language.

ISABEL .... My mother spoke Italian to me when I was young.

6

ISABEL I haven't got my own flat.

BERNIE .... I rent a place with a friend.

7

BERNIE I hate working at weekends.

HAYLEY ...., but I often do it.

8

HAYLEY I'm really hot.

BERNIE .... Can you open a window?

 Reading and Writing Portfolio 1 p64

9

2 Beginnings
Language Summary 2, Student's Book p121

2A Starting small

Past Simple G2.1

1 **a)** Complete the table with the infinitive or the Past Simple form of these verbs.

infinitive	Past Simple
1 *stay*	stayed
leave	2
3	read
close	4
5	wore
cry	6
7	stopped
fall	8
9	thought
make	10

b) Complete the table with the infinitive form of the verbs in **1a)**.

regular	irregular
1 *stay*	5 *leave*
2	6
3	7
4	8
	9
	10

2 **a)** Read the article about the people who started Ben & Jerry's ice-cream. Then put the verbs in brackets in the Past Simple.

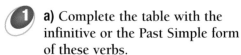

Ben & Jerry

Ben Cohen and Jerry Greenfield ¹ _met_ (meet) at school in New York in 1963. They both ² .... (have) the same hobby – food! When they finished school, they ³ .... (go) to college. But Ben ⁴ .... (not finish) his course and he ⁵ .... (get) a job selling ice-cream. In 1978, they both ⁶ .... (decide) to do a $5 course in making ice-cream. The course ⁷ .... (not be) difficult and the next year they ⁸ .... (start) their ice-cream business with their first shop: Ben & Jerry's, in Vermont, USA. On the first anniversary of Ben & Jerry's they ⁹ .... (give) everyone free ice-cream all day. Two years later, they ¹⁰ .... (open) their second shop, also in Vermont.

But Ben and Jerry ¹¹ .... only .... (not want) to make and sell ice-cream. So in 1985 they ¹² .... (begin) 'Ben & Jerry's Foundation', a charity to help poor people. Every year they give 7.5% of the company's money to the charity. By 2004 there ¹³ .... (be) more than 450 Ben & Jerry's shops in over 18 countries including France, Germany, Italy, Spain and Mexico. In the same year, we ¹⁴ .... (spend) over $300,000,000 on their ice-cream!

b) Write questions for these answers. Use the Past Simple.

1 When / Ben and Jerry / meet?

 When did Ben and Jerry meet?

 In 1963.

2 Who / get / a job selling ice-cream?

 ....

 Ben.

3 What happen / 1978?

 ....

 They did a course in ice-cream making.

4 When / they / open / their first shop?

 ....

 In 1979.

5 What / they / do / on their first anniversary?

....

They gave everyone free ice-cream all day.

6 Why / they / start / 'Ben & Jerry's Foundation'?

....

Because they wanted to help poor people.

7 How many shops / be / there in 2004?

....

There were more than 450.

8 How much / we / spend / on Ben & Jerry's ice-cream in 2004?

....

....

Over $300,000,000.

Past time phrases

3 Choose the correct words.

1 William Shakespeare was born in ⟨the sixteenth century⟩/ *sixteen years ago*.
2 *Last/In* month I couldn't speak any English!
3 I met my boyfriend on holiday *last/in* summer.
4 The first Kentucky Fried Chicken restaurant opened *in/on* 1952.
5 McDonald's opened its first restaurant in the *1940/forties*.
6 He is here somewhere. I saw him two minutes *ago/before*.
7 My parents got married twenty years *before/ago*.
8 I think she was here the day before *today/yesterday*.

 # 2B First meetings

Past Continuous: positive and negative G2.2

| *Ricky* | *Jade and Claude* | *Alison* | *Carl* | *Liz* | *Neal and Karen* |

1 **Look at the pictures. Then write what the people were doing at seven o'clock yesterday evening. Use the Past Continuous.**

> wait for a taxi   talk to a friend   jog in the park
> play on her computer   watch TV   think about his girlfriend

1 Ricky *was waiting for a taxi.*
2 Jade and Claude ....
3 Alison ....
4 Carl ....
5 Liz ....
6 Neal and Karen ....

2 Choose the correct words.

1 Pauline and her boyfriend ⟨*lived*⟩/ *were living* in China for three months.
2 We got married while my wife *did/ was doing* her degree at university.
3 Damon was looking out of the window when he *saw/was seeing* her.
4 When Nicole *heard/was hearing* the news, she quickly phoned her mother.
5 I *worked/was working* in Spain when I met my boyfriend.
6 The weather was good so we *walked/ were walking* home together.
7 This time last year they *went/were going* on dates and now they're married!
8 You *talked/were talking* to someone so I didn't want to say anything.

3 Read the article. Put the verbs in brackets in the Past Simple or Past Continuous.

In 1998, Alexandra Tolstoy ¹ _was working_ (work) in a bank, but she ² _was_ (be) bored. She decided to leave her job and ride across Central Asia on a horse for charity. When she ³ .... (meet) Shamil Galimzyanov for the first time, she ⁴ .... (travel) through Uzbekistan. She ⁵ .... (not feel) very well so she didn't notice him. But while they ⁶ .... (ride) their horses, they started talking. Alexandra ⁷ .... (think) Shamil was very interesting. His life was very different from her own. And soon she ⁸ .... (know) that she was falling in love with him.

Three years later Alexandra ⁹ .... (visit) Shamil in Uzbekistan again. At the time, she ¹⁰ .... (go out) with another man, but a few months later she ¹¹ .... (break up) with him.

Alexandra ¹² .... (get) engaged to Shamil in 2002 while she and her family ¹³ .... (stay) with him. They ¹⁴ .... (get) married in London and now they live in Moscow, in Russia.

4 **a)** Write questions about the article in **3**. Use the Past Continuous.

1 Where / Alexandra / work / in 1998?

   Where was Alexandra working in 1998?

2 Where / she / travel / when she met Shamil?

   ....

3 How / she / feel / when she met him?

   ....

4 What / Shamil and Alexandra / do / when they started talking?

   ....

5 / she / go out / with anyone when she went back to Uzbekistan?

   ....

6 Where / her family / stay / when they got engaged?

   ....

b) Write answers to the questions in **4a)**.

1 _She was working in a bank._

2 ....

3 ....

4 ....

5 ....

6 ....

Relationships (1) V2.2

5 Read the article in **3** again and complete the phrases.

1 get _married_ to someone

2 .... in .... with someone

3 .... engaged to someone

4 .... out .... someone

5 .... someone for the first ....

6 .... up .... someone

2C The 1001 Nights

VOCABULARY AND READING

Reading

1 Read the first paragraphs of two stories. Then put the stories in the correct order.

The Lazy Man in Love:

_h)_ , ... , ... , ...

The Man and his Two Girlfriends:

_c)_ , ... , ... , ...

a) They told the man to come back when he had a good job. So the man went to university, studied hard and soon he was working for a multinational company. He returned to her parents and asked again. They were very pleased and called their daughter.

b) When she saw him she always pulled out a few of the black hairs on his head. She wanted him to look older. So every time the man went to see his girlfriends he lost a few grey hairs and then a few black hairs.

c) There was once a man called Lothar. He was only thirty, but some of his hair was grey. Lothar had two girlfriends – one who was twenty years old and the other who was forty.

d) But when she saw her boyfriend in his suit and heard he was working in an office, she was very sad. 'You're not the man I loved,' she said. And she broke up with him immediately.

e) After a few years, the man had no hair on his head at all!

f) The man soon wanted to marry the girl so he decided to ask her parents. The girl's parents didn't want their daughter to marry him. How could he look after their daughter? He was unemployed!

g) The younger girlfriend was worried about going out with an older man. When she saw him, she always took out a few of his grey hairs. The older girlfriend was worried about going out with a younger man.

h) There was once a man called Otiose. He didn't have any money, but he was happy. One day he was lying on the beach when he saw a beautiful woman. He asked her out immediately and they went on a date.

2 Read the stories in 1 again. Are these sentences true (T) or false (F)? Correct the false sentences.

didn't want

1 F Otiose's girlfriend ~~wanted~~ him to get a job.

2 T Otiose was happy when he met his girlfriend.

3 ☐ At the start of the story Otiose had a job.

4 ☐ Lothar was older than both his girlfriends.

5 ☐ Lothar's girlfriends didn't like his hair.

6 ☐ At the end of the story Lothar became bald.

Connecting words (1) V2.3

3 Match beginnings of sentences 1–6 to endings a)–f). Use *so, because, while, when* or *until*.

1 Lothar's older girlfriend didn't like his black hairs _so_

2 Lothar's girlfriends pulled out his hair ....

3 Lothar's younger girlfriend pulled his grey hairs out ....

4 The girl's parents didn't want Otiose to marry her ....

5 Otiose met his girlfriend ....

6 Otiose didn't have a degree ....

a) he went to university.

b) he was lying on a beach.

c) he came to visit her.

d) he didn't have any left.

e) he didn't have a job.

f) she pulled them out.

13

Starting conversations RW2.1

1 Fill in the gaps with these phrases.

> ~~How do you know~~   Do you live   Didn't we meet in
> do you know   where did you meet   You're a teacher
> Are you a friend of   What do you do?

1 ANNA   Sid, this is Sarah.
   SID   Nice to meet you, Sarah.
   SARAH   You too.
           [1] *How do you know* Anna?
   SID   I work with her.
   SARAH   Oh. So [2] _____
           _____ Lucy Barker?
   SID   Yes. Why?
   SARAH   She's my sister. She couldn't come tonight.

2 TARA   Wow! There are a lot of
           people in here!
   JARED   Yes! It's coffee time. I'm
           Jared. I work downstairs.
           [3] _____
   TARA   Hi, I'm Tara. I'm an
           accountant.
   JARED   Oh really.
           [4] _____ in Cambridge?
   TARA   No, I live in London.

3 KATE   Hello. [5] _____
           Paddy's or Audrey's?
   MARK   Audrey's.
   KATE   Me too! Were you at
           university with her?
   MARK   No. Were you?
   KATE   Yes, I was. So [6] _____
           _____ her?
   MARK   At work. I went out with her, but she broke up with me
           when she met Paddy.

4 ROLAND   Hello. [7] _____
             Manchester last year?
   MAX   Manchester? Was it at the
         computer conference?
   ROLAND   Yes, you gave a talk about
             computers in education.
   MAX   Oh yes. [8] _____
         _____ at
         Bath College, aren't you?
   ROLAND   That's right.

Ending conversations RW2.2

2 **a)** Make sentences with these words to
complete the conversations.

a) A   I / meet / we / hope / soon / again .
        I hope we meet again soon.
    B   I'm sure we will.

b) A   you / meeting / was / It / nice .
        _____

    B   probably / you / again / See / here .
        _____

    A   Yes, bye.

c) A   again / was / It / nice / see / to / you .
        _____

    B   You too. I really enjoyed your talk
        last year.
    A   Thank you. Here's my email address.
        touch / Let's / in / keep .
        _____

d) A   you / maybe / soon / See .
        _____

    B   Are you going to their party tonight?
    A   Oh, yes. Of course.
    B   later / See / then / you !
        _____

b) Match the ends of conversations a)–d)
in **2a)** to conversations 1–4 in **1**.

1 *a)*   2 _____   3 _____   4 _____

 Reading and Writing Portfolio 2 p66

3 The world of work

Language Summary 3, Student's Book p123

3A Getting qualified

Employment V3.1

1 **a)** Match the words/phrases in A to the words/phrases in B.

A	B
1 a good	a) security
2 long	b) office
3 opportunities	c) holidays
4 my own	d) salary
5 friendly	e) for promotion
6 job	f) colleagues
7 a good	g) pay
8 flexible	h) training
9 opportunities	i) boss
10 holiday	j) pay
11 on-the-job	k) working hours
12 sick	l) for travel

b) Complete the sentences with a phrase from **1a)**.

1 I don't want to work at the same time every day. I'd like a job with *flexible working hours.*

2 I like going to different towns and countries so I'd like a job with ....

3 If I am ill, do I get .... ?

4 Teachers work very hard, but they often get .... in the summer.

5 I've got a lot of .... I like working with them.

6 Money is important to me so I'd like ....

have to/had to (1): positive and negative G3.1

2 Complete the sentences with *has to* and these verbs.

practise	take	know	work	be (x 2)

1 A musician *has to practise* a lot.

2 A shop assistant .... polite.

3 A doctor .... long hours.

4 An accountant .... good at maths.

5 A London taxi driver .... 25,000 streets.

6 A parent usually .... holidays when schools are closed.

3 Fill in the gaps with the positive or negative form of *have to*. Use the Present Simple or Past Simple.

1 Phil and Miriam get a good salary. They *don't have to* worry about money.

2 Matt works for himself. He .... get up early.

3 Leah and I can't come this weekend. We .... visit Leah's parents.

4 I don't have my own office. I .... share it with a colleague.

5 The company were very good to her when she was ill. They .... give her sick pay, but they did.

6 I have three small children so I .... have flexible working hours.

7 In the UK students .... do at least six years' training to become a doctor.

8 She .... come to work today. Why is she here?

have to/had to (2): questions and short answers `G3.2`

4 **a)** Fill in the gaps with *Do/Does/Did* and *have to*.

1   A   I work in a department store.

 B   _Do_ you _have to_ work on bank holidays?

2   A   Andy teaches English in Brazil.

 B   .... he .... speak Portuguese?

3   A   Nadia left a few minutes ago.

 B   But it's so early! .... she .... go?

4   A   Dad and I are going to see your grandmother on Sunday.

 B   .... we .... come?

5   A   I like this jacket, but it's a bit small.

 B   I'm sorry, but we haven't got any more in that colour. .... it .... be black?

6   A   I couldn't find my student card.

 B   Oh, dear. .... you .... pay full price?

b) Write short answers to the questions in 4a).

1   Yes, I _do_ . And it's always really busy.

2   No, he .... But he can.

3   Yes, she .... She said she was sorry.

4   No, you .... But she'd probably like to see you.

5   No, it .... What colours do you have in my size?

6   Yes, I .... It was £15!

3B Job-hunting

Looking for a job `V3.2`

1 **a)** Put sentences a)–l) in the correct order to make a story about Jez.

a) ☐ for an interview. But he said the job was

b) ☐ 1 My friend, Jez, is unemployed at the moment. He

c) ☐ benefit at first because he decided to take a holiday. But now he's looking

d) ☐ was working for a multinational company and he was

e) ☐ job. He didn't get unemployment

f) ☐ 12 find a job soon.

g) ☐ for about three jobs every week. He saw an interesting

h) ☐ for a new job. I helped him to write his CV and he applies

i) ☐ advert in the newspaper last week. He filled in the

j) ☐ earning a lot of money. But last month he lost his

k) ☐ application form and went

l) ☐ terrible – the people were really unfriendly. I'm sure he will

b) Find these phrases in 1a). Then write the infinitive form of the verb.

1   _apply_ for a job

2   .... unemployed

3   .... a lot of money

4   .... your job

5   .... unemployment benefit

6   .... a CV

7   .... for a job

8   .... in an application form

9   .... for an interview

10 .... a job

Present Continuous and Present Simple `G3.3`

2 **a)** Choose the correct words.

1   Miguel (never works)/is never working at weekends.

2   Mandy *is/is being* unemployed at the moment.

3   I *still learn/'m still learning* a lot in my job.

4   We *watch/'re watching* a film at the moment.

5   I *live/'m living* in France at the moment.

6   My parents *usually go/are usually going* on holiday in winter.

7   My brother *wants/is wanting* to live abroad.

8   What's wrong? Why *do you cry/are you crying*?

b) Match the sentences in **2a)** to their meanings.

a) Present Simple for routines: _1_ and _____ .

b) Present Simple for states: _____ and _____ .

c) Present Continuous for things that are happening at the moment of speaking: _____ and _____ .

d) Present Continuous for things that are temporary or are happening around now: _____ and _____ .

3 Look at the pictures. Then fill in the gaps with the Present Simple or Present Continuous form of these verbs.

| ~~teach~~ | ~~learn~~ | ~~work~~ | lose | win | stay |
| relax | cycle | drive | be | rain | go |

1 Helen _teaches_ French, but today she _'s learning_ Italian.

2 Cliff and Sue usually _work_ hard, but today they _____ .

3 Brian often _____ to work, but today he _____ .

4 It _____ generally sunny, but today it _____ .

5 For holidays we usually _____ camping, but this year we _____ in a hotel.

6 I always _____ at tennis, but today I _____ .

4 Read the article and put the verbs in brackets in the Present Simple or Present Continuous.

Top tips for finding a **new** job

[1] _Are_ you _looking_ (look) for a new job? Well, you [2] _____ (read) this article so the answer is probably yes!

- Your CV [3] _____ (be) an advert for you! I always [4] _____ (ask) a friend to read my application forms or CV. [5] _____ you _____ (learn) anything new at the moment? I [6] _____ (study) Spanish. I [7] _____ (not need) Spanish for my job, but it's a useful language. And it looks good on my CV!

- Before interviews, I [8] _____ (try) to find out something about the company. Most large companies [9] _____ (have) websites. My daughter [10] _____ (want) to work for Microsoft in the future and at the moment she [11] _____ (read) a book about the company.

- I always [12] _____ (arrive) five or ten minutes early for an interview. While I [13] _____ (wait), I [14] _____ (read) my notes carefully.

- In an interview, you [15] _____ (need) to listen very carefully and answer the questions honestly. And smile! It [16] _____ (help) you relax!

17

3C Strange jobs

Word building (1): noun endings V3.3

1 Do the puzzle. Find the job (↓).

1 politics	6 violin
2 write	7 clean
3 assist	8 direct
4 paint	9 cook
5 music	10 act

↓

1 P O L I T I C I A N

2 **a)** Are these words nouns, verbs or both? Write N (noun), V (verb) or B (both).

1 [N] collection

2 [ ] laugh

3 [ ] advertise

4 [ ] visit

5 [ ] cyclist

6 [ ] paint

b) Put the words in **2a)** in the table. Then complete the table with the missing nouns or verbs.

noun	verb
collection	collect

Reading

3 **a)** Read an interview with a police diver. Write questions 1–5 in the correct places A–E.

1 Where did you learn about diving for the police?
2 What qualities do you need in your work?
3 What do you do as a police diver?
4 How did you become interested in diving?
5 Have you got any diving qualifications?

A _How did you become interested in diving?_

When I was young my parents lived in Honduras, Central America. I did my first serious dive when I was ten with my mother and father. I can remember it now. My parents had an [1] _argument_ (argue) about it. My mother thought I was too young. My father said it was her [2] _____ (decide) so she came with us!

B _____

Yes. When I was 18, I took a diving [3] _____ (examine) and became a professional diver. The [4] _____ (examine) said I was born to be a diver!

C _____

While I was at university I saw an [5] _____ (advertise) for the police in a newspaper. I applied and I got an interview. The [6] _____ (interview) was a police diver and we [7] _____ (discuss) our experiences. I knew then I wanted to be a police diver. I trained as a policeman first and then I did a special training course to become a police diver. It was really difficult!

D _____

People usually think police divers have to look for bodies all the time. It isn't true! My job is never the same and I love the [8] _____ (excite). We examine plane crashes, look in rivers for knives or guns and we often have to rescue people at sea.

E _____

Well you need to be an excellent [9] _____ (swim), of course. And you have to be physically strong – diving in English rivers and canals is not like diving in the Caribbean Ocean – it can be very cold, very dark and very smelly!

b) Read the interview again and fill in the gaps with the correct form of the words in brackets.

3D I'm really sorry!

Apologies, reasons and promises RW3.1

1 a) Match apologies 1–4 to reasons a)–d).

1 Sorry, I couldn't come to your party. _d)_

2 I'm sorry I couldn't get the DVD you wanted. ......

3 I'm really sorry, but I can't give you the report today. ......

4 Sorry, I can't play football on Wednesday. ......

a) The shop didn't have it so I had to order one on the Internet.

b) I have to go to the doctor's – my knee hurts.

c) My computer crashed so I have to write it again.

d) It was my mum's birthday on Saturday so I had to go and see her.

b) Now match the promises to each sentence in **1a)**.

a) I'll try and visit soon. _1_

b) I'll tell you when it arrives. ......

c) I'll play next week. ......

d) I'll finish it tomorrow. ......

2 Put the conversation in the correct order.

a)	☐ MARION	Yes. And you'll remember your phone!
b)	☐ NATE	I left my phone at home and I didn't have your number.
c)	☐ MARION	Oh, dear. Why didn't you call?
d)	1 NATE	I'm really sorry I couldn't come to the meeting this morning.
e)	☐ MARION	You didn't have the number? This was an important meeting, Nate.
f)	☐ NATE	I know. Next time I'll take a taxi.
g)	☐ MARION	What happened? We waited for you.
h)	☐ NATE	The 8.15 train was cancelled and I had to wait for the next one.

3 Fill in the gaps with *'ll*, *can't*, *couldn't*, *have to* or *had to*.

1 I'm really sorry, but I _couldn't_ find your keys.

I .... look again when I get home.

2 Sorry, I .... send you the document now. My computer isn't working, but I .... find an Internet café.

3 I .... work tonight so I .... meet you. Are you busy tomorrow?

4 Sorry, I .... call Mr Travis yesterday. I .... look after the Japanese visitors all day. I .... ring him this afternoon.

4 Look at the table and write sentences.

apology	reason	promise
1 couldn't call the builder today	work late	call him tomorrow
2 can't meet you later	visit my parents	see you at the weekend
3 couldn't go to meeting yesterday	go on a training course	come to the next meeting
4 can't work on Saturday	go to the doctor	work late next week

1 *I'm sorry, but I couldn't call the builder today. I had to work late. I'll call him tomorrow.*

2 ....

....

3 ....

....

4 ....

....

Review: spelling

5 **S** Choose the correct words.

1 *beautifull*/*beautiful*

2 *writting*/*writing*

3 *swimmer*/*swimer*

4 *gallery*/*galery*

5 *developped*/*developed*

6 *shopping*/*shoping*

7 *openned*/*opened*

8 *looses*/*loses*

9 *opportunities*/*oportunities*

10 *success*/*succes*

 Reading and Writing Portfolio 3 p68

4 That's entertainment!

Language Summary 4, Student's Book p126

 The silver screen

Types of film V4.1

1 Fill in the gaps with these words.

> ~~love story~~   western   science-fiction film
> horror film   musical   historical drama
> romantic comedy   comedy   war film

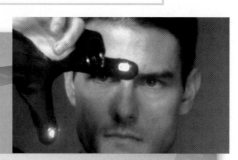

FILM CHOICE

Next time you rent a video or DVD, look out for these film classics!

Brief Encounter Laura Jesson meets Doctor Alec Harvey. They are married, but they continue to meet every week at a station. This is a beautiful, but sad [1] *love story.*

Forrest Gump Tom Hanks is very funny in this wonderful [2] .... Hanks won his second Oscar for his acting.

Minority Report In the year 2054, the police can see the future. Tom Cruise is policeman John Anderton in this exciting [3] ....

The Blues Brothers Jake and his brother, Elwood, decide to play their last concert. An exciting [4] .... with songs from Aretha Franklin.

Elizabeth This [5] .... tells the interesting story of the English queen, Elizabeth I (1558–1603).

Apocalypse Now Captain Willard is looking for Colonel Kutz in Cambodia in 1969. Francis Ford Coppola directs this classic [6] ....

Win a Date with Tad Hamilton! In a competition, Rosalee wins a date with Tad Hamilton, a good-looking and famous actor. Will they fall in love? A simple, but very funny [7] ....

Little Big Man An old man tells the story of his life. There are cowboys, Indians and everything you expect in this classic [8] ....

Psycho Don't watch this alone! A woman stops at a lonely hotel in Alfred Hitchcock's famous [9] ....

Review: past forms and past participles

2 Complete the table.

infinitive	Past Simple	past participle
1 be	*was* or	
2 cry		
3 do		
4 go		or
5 have		
6 hear		
7 meet		
8 stop		
9 watch		
10 write		

Present Perfect for life experiences (1): positive and negative G4.1

3 Look at the information about film directors. Fill in the gaps with the correct form of the Present Perfect.

	Joshua	Mar	Ren
write a film	✗	✓	✓
make a short film	✗	✓ three	✓
meet a famous director	✓ Woody Allen	✗	✗
go to Hollywood	✓	✓	✗

1 Joshua *hasn't written* a film.

2 Ren and Mar *have written* a film.

3 Joshua .... a short film.

4 Mar .... three short films.

5 Joshua .... a famous director, Woody Allen.

6 Mar and Ren .... any famous directors.

7 Joshua and Mar .... to Hollywood.

8 Ren .... to Hollywood.

4 Fill in the gaps with these verbs. Use the Present Perfect and if possible, contractions (*'s, 've*).

see	broke	drive	learn
fail	try	go	use

1 My daughter *'s seen* all the Harry Potter films.

2 Nathan .... never .... a foreign language.

3 I .... never .... a mobile phone.

4 We .... Japanese food. Is it good?

5 You .... never .... an exam!

6 I .... my arm twice.

7 Raoul and I .... on holiday three times this year.

8 You .... abroad.

5 Put the verbs in brackets in the Present Perfect or Past Simple.

Sofia Coppola is the daughter of Francis Ford Coppola, the film director. She [1] *was* (be) born in 1971 and she [2] .... (appear) in her first film, *The Godfather*, in 1972. In her career she [3] .... (act) in over 15 films including *Star Wars Episode 1* with Ewan McGregor. But most of all, she enjoys writing and directing films. When she [4] .... (be) 18 she [5] .... (write) a story, *Life without Zoë*, for the film *New York Stories*. In 2003 she [6] .... (direct) her most famous film, *Lost in Translation*. A year later she [7] .... (win) an Oscar for the film. Now, three people in the Coppola family [8] .... (win) Oscars! Of course, this isn't all Sofia [9] .... (do) in her life. She [10] .... (design) clothes and she [11] .... (start) her own fashion company. Amazing for someone in her early thirties.

4B The rhythm of life

Music V4.2

1 Do the puzzle. Find the type of music (↓).

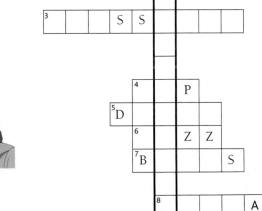

1 R A P
2 _ G G
3 _ S S
4 P
5 D
6 Z Z
7 B S
8 A
9 R K
10 R

Present Perfect for life experiences (2): questions with *ever* G4.2

 a) Write questions with these words.

1 / Steffie / ever / write / a song?

Has Steffie ever written a song?

2 / Bob Dylan / ever / have / a number one in the UK?

....

....

3 / you / ever / buy / a CD on the Internet?

....

....

4 / you and Abby / ever / hear / of the band Coldplay?

....

....

5 / Cory and Amy / ever / sing / karaoke?

....

....

6 / your brother / ever / play / in a band?

....

....

b) Write short answers to the questions in **2a)**.

1 Yes, *she has.*   4 No, ...

2 No, ...   5 Yes, ...

3 Yes, ...   6 No, ...

Review: Present Perfect and Past Simple

 Choose the correct answers, a), b) or c).

1 He's never .... me flowers.

a) give   (b) given   c) gave

2 She .... my birthday last year.

a) forgot   b) forgotten   c) forget

3 Did he .... out at the weekend?

a) been   b) went   c) go

4 A Did you watch television yesterday?
  B Yes, I ....

a) have   b) watched   c) did

5 They .... skiing.

a) 've never been   b) 've never went
c) never been

 Fill in the gaps. Use the verbs in brackets and the Present Perfect or the Past Simple. Use contractions ('s, 've) if possible.

1 A *Have* you ever *seen* (see) an opera?

  B No, I .... What about you?

  A Yes, I ....

  B What .... you .... (see)?

  A Carmen. It .... (be) about four hours long!

2 A .... you and Dan ever .... (be) to a karaoke bar?

  B Yes, we .... What about you and Will?

  A No, we .... What was it like?

  B I .... (hate) it, but Dan .... (love) it!

3 A .... you ever .... (use) an MP3 player?

  B Yes, I .... I .... (buy) one last year.

  A Me too. Where .... you .... (buy) it?

  B I .... (order) one on the Internet. It .... (cost) about £80.

4 A .... Gwen ever .... (lose) anything important?

  B Yes, she .... ! She .... (lose) our tickets to a Robbie Williams concert.

  A What .... you .... (do)?

  B We .... (try) to buy some more, but we .... (not can).

  A So, ... you ever .... (see) him in concert?

  B No, I .... !

4C TV or not TV?

TV nouns and verbs V4.3

1 Write the TV words.

1 You need a DV_D_ player to play a DVD.

2 T_ _   _ _ _ _ is a programme about important events.

3 "Dinner's ready. T_ _ _   _ _ _ the TV!"

4 The most famous r_ _ _ _ _ _   _ _ programme is *Big Brother*.

5 On a c_ _ _   s_ _ _ , famous people answer questions about themselves.

6 "I want to watch that programme later. Can you r_ _ _ _ _ it?"

7 D_ _ _ _ _ _ _ _ _ _ _ _ are factual programmes about real situations or people.

8 S_ _ _   o_ _ _ _ _ are popular programmes on TV every week.

Reading

2 Find the numbers in the article. What do they describe?

a) 94% *By 1950, 94% of Americans had a radio in their house.*

b) 66% _____

c) 30 million _____

d) 650 million _____

e) at least 200 _____

blogsociety.net

prev thread
next thread

In 1935 the radio was very popular. Families sat down every night and listened to dramas. By 1950, 94% of Americans had a radio in their house. But by 1955, 66% of American houses had their own TV.

And now we have the Internet. In 1996, about 30 million people used the Internet. In 2005, there were over 650 million people online. They buy books, send emails and now many watch TV – there are at least 200 TV channels on the Internet. Will the Internet kill TV?

-ed and *-ing* adjectives V4.4

3 **a)** Read four responses to the article and choose the correct words.

This is a [1]*worrying/worried* article. I work for a company that makes TVs. But I think TV is going to be here for a long time. Remember, 90% of people in the world have never used a computer.
Chas, New York

_____

I was [2]*surprising/surprised* by something I read recently: people who use the Internet watch over four hours less TV every week than people who don't use the Internet. TV is dying! This is [3]*exciting/excited* news!
Hugo, São Paolo

_____

I'm living in the UK at the moment. Internet TV is [4]*amazing/amazed*. I can watch [5]*interesting/interested* programmes in my first language – Chinese.
Wei-Sum Leung, London

_____

In our house, we have two TVs, two computers and five children. In the past, the children argued over the remote control. Now they fight to use the computer! They think TV is [6]*boring/bored* and they are [7]*tiring/tired* of watching it.
Claudia, Rome

b) Read the responses in **3a)** again. Are the sentences true (T) or false (F)?

1 | F | 90% of people in the world have got a computer.

2 | | Chas thinks that television isn't going to die soon.

3 | | People who use the Internet watch four hours of television a week.

4 | | Hugo prefers watching television to the Internet.

5 | | Wei-Sum watches Chinese television on the Internet.

6 | | Claudia's children love watching television.

4D What do you think?

Agreeing, disagreeing, and asking for opinions RW4.1

1 Fill in the gaps with these phrases.

> I'm sorry I don't agree   Yes, maybe you're right
> What do you think   Do you agree with that
> No, definitely not

1 TREVOR I think university is a waste of time.

  NIKKI [1] *I'm sorry I don't agree.* A university degree
  is important for some jobs.
  [2] _____ ,
  Trevor?

  TREVOR [3] _____ .
  Young people need experience. Not books!

2 RUSS There are children in here. Smokers should
  go outside.

  JOHN [4] _____ .
  But it is a party.
  [5] _____ Tessa?

  TESSA Perhaps we should open a window.

> I'm not sure about that   Do you think
> Yes, definitely   What about you   I agree with

3 KELVIN [6] _____
  living in the country is more relaxing?

  JEN [7] _____ .
  I hate the noise of the city.

4 ALLIE I think everyone should have satellite
  television.

  INGRID [8] _____ .
  My children watch too much television
  already!

  ALLIE Well, you can always turn the TV off!
  [9] _____ ,
  Dale? What do you think?

  DALE [10] _____
  Ingrid. Satellite television is just more chat
  shows and more reality TV programmes.
  Rubbish – all of them!

2 **a)** Match conversations 1–4 in **1** to people A–D in
the picture.

1 _A_   2 _____   3 _____   4 _____

b) Complete the table with the phrases in **1**.

asking opinion	agreeing	disagreeing
1 *What do you think?*	5	8
2	6	9
3	7	10
4		

3 Do you agree or disagree with these sentences?
Choose a phrase from **2b)**.

1 It's better to live in the city than the country.
  I don't agree./I'm not sure about that.

2 Everyone should have satellite television.
  _____

3 Smokers should smoke outside.
  _____

4 University is a waste of time.
  _____

 Reading and Writing Portfolio 4 p70

5 Into the future

Language Summary 5, Student's Book p128

5A Man or machine?

Verb-noun collocations (1) V5.1

1 **a)** Match verbs 1–7 to words/phrases a)–g).

1	do	a)	the cats
2	clean	b)	cars
3	feed	c)	the carpets
4	look like	d)	me
5	look after	e)	the world
6	build	f)	the housework
7	take over	g)	my brother

b) Fill in the gaps with the phrases in **1a)**.

WOULD YOU LIKE A ROBOT?
We asked five people the same question.

please! I hate ¹ _doing the housework_ so
² _____ and
s like that. And when we go on holiday, it
_____ !

Can it ⁴ _____
when my parents are out? He never listens
to me – maybe he will listen to a robot.

ave lots of robots at our factory. They help
_____ . So, no!
't want one at home.

No, thank you! Robots are going to
⁶ _____ one
day. I saw a documentary about that once.

I want a robot that ⁷ _____
_____ . It can go to work
while I stay in bed!

will for prediction; might; will be able to G5.1

2 **a)** Make sentences about the future with these words.

1 email / Everyone / address / an / have / will .
   Everyone will have an email address.

2 work / will / Lots of / home / at / people .
   _____

3 electricity / Cars / will / only use .
   _____

4 government / have / will / Europe / one .
   _____

b) Fill in the gaps with *won't* and these verbs.

~~need~~ use send be

a) People _won't need_ to travel to work.

b) We _____ any letters by post.

c) There _____ as many countries.

d) Cars _____ petrol.

c) Match the sentences in **2a)** to the sentences in **2b)**.

1 _b)_   2 _____   3 _____   4 _____

3 **a)** Fill in the gaps with *will*, *won't* and the verbs in brackets.

1 A England _won't win_ the next World Cup. (win)

 B Do you think Brazil _will win_ ? (win)

2 A In 10 years, we _____ CDs in the shops. (buy)

 B _____ we _____ them on the Internet? (buy)

3 A You _____ the exam. (pass)

 B _____ I _____ to take it again? (be able)

4 A I _____ here tomorrow. (be)

 B Do you think you _____ on Friday? (come)

b) Write short answers to the questions in **3a)**.

1 Yes, I _do_ .   3 No, you _____ .

2 Yes, we _____ .   4 No, I _____ .

25

4 A group of school children made predictions about the future. Rewrite the sentences with *might*.

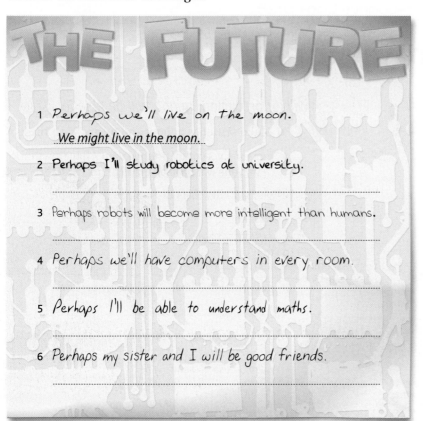

THE FUTURE

1 Perhaps we'll live on the moon.

We might live in the moon.

2 Perhaps I'll study robotics at university.

_____

3 Perhaps robots will become more intelligent than humans.

_____

4 Perhaps we'll have computers in every room.

_____

5 Perhaps I'll be able to understand maths.

_____

6 Perhaps my sister and I will be good friends.

_____

 5 Fill in the gaps with *can* or *'ll/will be able to*.

1 By next year I ＿*'ll be able to*＿ speak English very well.

2 We ＿＿＿＿＿ travel to the moon now, but in the future we ＿＿＿＿＿ live there.

3 When ＿＿＿＿＿ robots ＿＿＿＿＿ move around easily?

4 In 20 years, I don't think you ＿＿＿＿＿ drive a car in many capital cities.

5 In 50 years computers ＿＿＿＿＿ think like humans.

6 My eight-month-old son ＿＿＿＿＿ already say a few words. In a year he ＿＿＿＿＿ talk.

 # Never too old ─────────────

Verb-noun collocations (2) V5.2

 1 **a)** Match the beginnings of sentences 1–8 to endings a)–h).

1 I'm sure you'll have ＿*d)*＿

2 Pam and Edgar are living ＿＿＿

3 My father loves taking ＿＿＿

4 Pat and I are looking forward to ＿＿＿

5 I think he did ＿＿＿

6 Our grandmother wants to learn ＿＿＿

7 Before university we spent ＿＿＿

8 We want to lie on a beach and get ＿＿＿

a) abroad at the moment.

b) a degree in maths, but I'm not sure.

c) how to use the Internet.

d) a great time in Italy.

e) spending more time with our grandchildren.

f) a suntan.

g) photos with his new digital camera.

h) a year travelling around the world.

b) Find these phrases in 1a). Then write the infinitive form of the verb.

1 ＿*have*＿ a great time

2 ＿＿＿ abroad

3 ＿＿＿ photos

4 ＿＿＿ time with someone

5 ＿＿＿ a degree

6 ＿＿＿ how to do something

7 ＿＿＿ time doing something

8 ＿＿＿ a suntan

Future plans and ambitions:
be going to G5.2

 2 Change the incorrect words in **bold**.

       are you

A When ¹**you are** going to retire?

B I'm going to ²**retired** next month.

A Are you going to ³**learned** anything new?

B I don't know, but I ⁴**not am** going to do anything difficult.

A Is your wife ⁵**going retire**?

B Yes, she ⁶**going**. Next year.

A And ⁷**what you** going to do then?

B I'm going to ⁸**spending** a lot more time out of the house!

3 Choose the best meaning for each sentence.

1 We're looking forward to meeting you.
- a) We're going to enjoy meeting you.
- b) We're thinking of meeting you.
- c) We might enjoy meeting you.

2 I'm planning to live abroad.
- a) I might live abroad.
- b) I'd like to live abroad.
- c) I'm going to live abroad.

3 He's hoping to retire early.
- a) He's going to retire early.
- b) He'd like to retire early.
- c) He's sure he will retire early.

4 I'm thinking of buying a computer.
- a) I might buy a new computer.
- b) I'm going to buy a new computer.
- c) I'm planning to buy a new computer.

 4 Read about five people's plans. Then fill in the gaps in sentences 1–10.

LORNA I might retire early. I don't know. I'm 55 now and my husband retired last year. He spends most of his time in the garden. I'd really like to be there with him. I'm definitely going to learn a new language. I hate going abroad and speaking English.

CASS I'm only 26 so I'm not going to retire soon! Jamie and I are going to have a baby next year and we're really excited about that. We want to have a big family and live in a big house. Then my children and grandchildren will all be able to stay.

SUE Well, Roger and I don't agree about this. I love work and I don't want to retire! I know I won't have anything to do.

ROGER I asked my boss at work recently and I might be able to retire next year. We might buy a house in France. I'd like to live there one day.

1 Lorna is thinking of __*retiring*__ early.

2 She's looking forward to .... more time with her husband.

3 She's planning to .... a new language.

4 Cass and Jamie are planning to .... a big family.

5 They're looking forward to .... their first child.

6 Cass would like to .... in a big house.

7 Sue isn't looking forward to ....

8 Sue is sure she will .... bored.

9 Roger is hoping to .... early.

10 They're thinking of .... a house in France.

Out of this world

Reading: verbs and prepositions V5.3

1 **a)** Read the article and write the correct names.

1 NASA's first spaceships to land on Mars. ....

2 Europe's first spaceship to go to Mars. ....

3 Dr Pillinger's first robot to go to Mars. ....

4 The robot Dr Pillinger wants to build next. ....

b) Read the article again and choose the correct words.

Dr Pillinger and a model of Beagle 2

The search for life on Mars started seriously in 1976. In that year two NASA (North American Space Agency) spaceships, Viking 1 and Viking 2, flew ¹*from/to* Mars and landed on the planet. In 1997 NASA returned ²*to/from* Mars and took over 20,000 photographs of the planet.

In the same year ESA (European Space Agency) decided to send their first spaceship to Mars – *Mars Express*. A British space scientist, Dr Colin Pillinger, heard about the mission. He had an idea: he could build a robot to travel ³*by/to* Mars inside ESA's spaceship. The robot could land on Mars and look for life on the planet.

In 1998, ESA agreed ⁴*with/about* Dr Pillinger's plan. Pillinger chose the name *Beagle 2* for the robot, after Charles Darwin's 1831 ship, *Beagle*.

Beagle 2 needed ⁵*to/for* send the Earth a signal when it landed. The signal tells scientists on Earth that the spaceship landed safely. Dr Pillinger asked a famous pop group, Blur, to write a song – the first pop concert on Mars!

Dr Pillinger and his team spent $60 million ⁶*for/on* the robot. And on Christmas Day 2003 everyone was looking forward ⁷*on/to* hearing Blur's song when the robot landed on Mars. The scientists waited ... and waited. But they didn't hear the song. They tried to contact the robot, but they never discovered the problem. And now they know they never will.

Now Dr Pillinger is talking ⁸*about/to* sending another robot to Mars in 2009. He has written to NASA because he wants the robot – called *Beagle 3*, of course – to travel inside a NASA spaceship. Good luck, Dr Pillinger!

c) Fill in the gaps with the correct question words. Then choose the correct answers.

1 *How many* spaceships did NASA send to Mars in 1976?

a) One.
b) Two. ⟵
c) Three.

2 .... did ESA decide to send a spaceship to Mars?

a) In 1976.
b) In 1997.
c) In 1998.

3 .... travelled on a ship called *Beagle*?

a) NASA.
b) Charles Darwin.
c) Dr Colin Pillinger.

4 .... wrote a song for Dr Pillinger's robot?

a) Dr Pillinger and his team.
b) A pop group.
c) A scientist.

5 .... happened to Dr Pillinger's robot?

a) We don't know.
b) It crashed on Mars.
c) It didn't take off.

6 .... does Dr Pillinger want *Beagle 3* to go to Mars?

a) Alone.
b) Inside *Mars Express 2*.
c) Inside NASA's next spaceship.

5D It's for charity

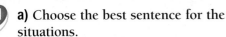

Offers, suggestions and requests RW5.1

1 **a)** Choose the best sentence for the situations.

1 You want to raise some money for a local charity. You think a quiz night is a good idea. You say:
   a) Shall I have a quiz night?
   b) Why don't we have a quiz night?
   c) I'll have a quiz night.

2 You want to advertise your charity event. Your brother works for a local newspaper. You say:
   a) I'll talk to my brother.
   b) Will you talk to your brother?
   c) Why don't we ask your brother?

3 You are organising a charity disco. You have a lot of CDs. You say:
   a) Shall I bring some CDs?
   b) Could you bring some CDs?
   c) Shall we buy some CDs?

4 Your mother is carrying some heavy bags of shopping. Your mother says:
   a) Let's carry these bags.
   b) Could you give you me a hand?
   c) Can I carry these bags for you?

5 You and your friend are lost and you don't have a map. Your friend says:
   a) Can I give you a hand?
   b) Shall we look at the map?
   c) Let's ask someone.

b) Choose the best response for the situations in **1a)**.

1 *Yes, why not?*/Great, thanks a lot.
2 *No, don't worry. Thanks anyway./*
   Great, thanks a lot.
3 *Yes, that'd be great./Yes, of course.*
4 *Yes, that'd be great./Yes, of course.*
5 *No, don't worry. Thanks anyway./*
   Yes, why not?

2 **a)** Read the article about Comic Relief and answer these questions.

1 Who started Comic Relief? ....
2 What happens on 'Red Nose Day'? ....
3 How much money have they raised so far? ....

In 1985 a group of comedians set up the charity Comic Relief. They wanted to use comedy and laughter to raise money for the world's poorest countries. Every two years they organise 'Red Nose Day'. Millions of people wear red noses while they raise money for the charity! So far, Comic Relief has raised almost £250 million.

b) Choose the correct words.

KAY   We're going to have a film night for Comic Relief. What films are we going to show?
STEVE ¹*Let's* /Why don't have some comedy films.
KAY   Yes, of course. ²*Will you/I'll* choose some?
STEVE Yes. I've got lots of DVDs.
DEB   ³*Shall I/I'll* help you if you like.
STEVE Great, thanks a lot. ⁴*I'll/Can I* do anything else?
KAY   Yes. We need a place to show the films.
DEB   Why ⁵*do/don't* we use my house? I have a big living room.
KAY   Yes, that'd ⁶*be/been* great.

3 Rewrite the sentences with the words in brackets.

1 Can you look after your brother?
   Will you look after your brother? (will)

2 We could ask Keiko.
   .... (why)

3 I want to go to Poland.
   .... (let's)

4 Let's go out this evening
   .... (shall)

5 Could you help me?
   Could .... (hand)

6 Will you make dinner?
   .... (can)

7 Do you want me to buy some tickets?
   .... (shall)

8 Could you do the washing up?
   .... (will)

 Reading and Writing Portfolio 5 p72

29

6 Family and friends

Language Summary 6, Student's Book p130

6A Life with teenagers

Character adjectives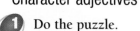

1 Do the puzzle.

```
¹O   ²        ³
 R
 G        ⁴
⁵A
 N
 I
 S
 E   ⁶
 D
     ⁷   ⁸
 
 ⁹
```

Across →

2 Laura finds it difficult to talk to strangers.

5 Julia wants a promotion and then she'll go to a bigger company.

6 They're only teenagers, but they behave like adults.

7 Clara always says please and thank you.

9 She's sometimes happy, but she's often unhappy and unfriendly.

Down ↓

1 She always plans her time very carefully.

2 I tried to talk to Terry, but he won't change his mind. He's not coming.

3 I've never met a person as kind and helpful.

4 I believe him – he always tells the truth.

8 He hasn't done any work today. He didn't do much yesterday!

Making comparisons

2 Complete the table with the correct form of these adjectives.

~~bright~~	polite	good	happy	patient	moody	hot
bad	difficult	new	funny	wet	big	far	old

-er	-y → -i + -er	double consonant + -er	more + adjective	irregular
brighter				

3 **a)** Fill in the gaps with the adjective in brackets or its comparative form.

You've heard your grandparents say this many times: life was different when I was young! But how?

I think life is ¹ _harder_ (hard) for teenagers now. We weren't as ² .... (worried) as they are about school or jobs. I think we were less ³ .... (ambitious). Teenagers have to be much ⁴ .... (organised) these days. I'm pleased I'm not a teenager today!

I don't think teenagers are much different than we were. They're as ⁵ .... (selfish) and as ⁶ .... (stubborn) as we were!

Betty   *May*   *Frank*

They're much ⁷ .... (impatient) than we were. They want everything and they want it now! We were a lot ⁸ .... (helpful) about things in the house – my grandchildren never do any cleaning or tidy their rooms. There is always something ⁹ .... (interesting) to do. And they certainly aren't as ¹⁰ .... (polite) as we were – we listened to our parents.

b) Fill in the gaps with the adjectives in brackets and (*not*) *as … as*.

1 Betty thinks teenagers …

  a) were _not as ambitious as_ (ambitious) they are now.

  b) didn't have to be _____ (organised) they do now.

2 Frank thinks teenagers …

  were _____ (selfish) they are now.

3 May thinks …

  a) her grandchildren are _____ (helpful) she was.

  b) teenagers are _____ (polite) they were.

 4 Make sentences a) and b) the same. Complete the sentences in b).

1 **a)** This doctor is more patient than my last one.

  b) My last doctor wasn't _as patient as this one._

2 **a)** This exercise is more difficult than the other ones.

  b) The other exercises aren't as _____ _____ .

3 **a)** Their children are much more polite than ours.

  b) Their children are a lot _____ _____ .

4 **a)** I'm not as interested in football as my brother.

  b) I'm less _____ _____ .

5 **a)** Gina is a little taller than her sister.

  b) Gina's sister is a bit _____ _____ .

6 **a)** I'm much less selfish than I was a few years ago.

  b) I'm a lot more _____ _____ .

 # Roles people play

Relationships (2) V6.2

 Complete the table with the correct words.

male	female
uncle	1 *aunt*
2	niece
grandfather	3
cousin	4
father-in-law	5
6	stepdaughter
7	ex-wife

 Fill in the gaps with these words.

> ex-boyfriend   close friend   brother-in-law   stepfather
> flatmate   relative   colleague   neighbour

1 Chloë's _ex-boyfriend_ was really selfish. They broke up because she wanted someone more considerate.

2 I have family all over the world. I even have a _____ in Canada, but I've never met him.

3 Shane is a very _____ of mine. We met at primary school.

4 My _____ is very easy to live with. She's tidy and often cleans the flat.

5 My _____ loves loud music. I can hear it through the walls every evening!

6 Our mother got married again when we were quite young, so we've always called my _____ Dad.

7 My _____ is quite wealthy. But when he and my sister got married, they were poor students!

8 I'll be home late tonight. A _____ is leaving and there's a small party at the office.

Superlatives `G6.2`

 a) Match types of adjectives 1–4 to rules a)–d).

type of adjective	rule
1 one-syllable adjectives: *hard*	a) put *most* before the adjective
2 one-syllable adjectives ending in -e: *safe*	b) change -*y* to -*i* and add -*est*
3 two-syllable adjectives ending in -*y*: *lazy*	c) add -*st*
4 other two-syllable and longer adjectives: *popular*	d) add -*est*

b) Match the adjectives to a rule in **3a)** and write the superlatives.

adjectives	rule	superlatives
angry	*b)*	*angriest*
pretty		
polite		
aggressive		
bright		
rich		
strange		
nice		

 Choose the correct words.

1 Jason is the least (busy)/busiest person in the family, of course.

2 Adrian is the *elder/eldest* person in the family.

3 Gemma is the *less/least* helpful person, but she will change.

4 Sean is the least *stress/stressed* person I know.

5 Sean is my *closest/most close* friend.

6 Joseph is the least *lazy/laziest* person.

7 The *brighter/brightest* person is Elaine – my mother.

8 I don't think I am the *less/least* organised person in the world.

 5 Look at Molly's family tree. Then fill in the gaps with the superlative form of these adjectives. Use *the* if necessary.

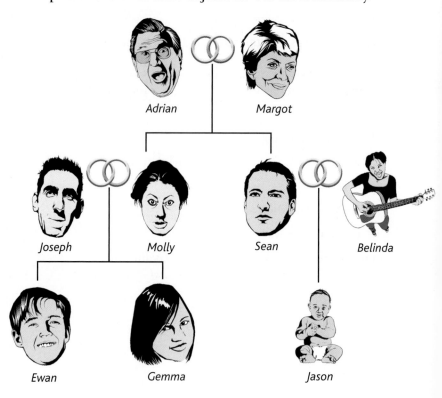

Adrian   Margot

Joseph   Molly   Sean   Belinda

Ewan   Gemma   Jason

intelligent	young	good	stubborn	happy
funny	thin	organised	musical	busy

MOLLY Well, let's start with my parents. I think my mother is [1] *the most intelligent* person in the family. She teaches at a university. But my father is certainly [2] .... – I laugh a lot when I'm with him.

My brother has always been my [3] .... friend. I can talk to him about anything. He's married to [4] .... person in our family. She plays the piano beautifully and she can sing. Their son is certainly [5] .... – he's only eleven months old.

My husband is [6] .... person in the family. He goes jogging a lot. He's also probably [7] .... person. He works for himself and never stops! Our son, is definitely our [8] .... child – he never stops smiling – like his grandfather. Gemma is only eight, but she's [9] .... child I've ever met. She always wants to do things her way. And me? Well, I'm not the [10] .... mother in the world, but I try!

6C Family Business

Prefixes and opposites of adjectives: un-, in-, im-, dis- **V6.3**

1 Fill in the gaps with a prefix from A and an adjective from B.

A	B	
un-	patient	correct
in-	honest	possible
im-	selfish	healthy
dis-	~~reliable~~	mature

1 A He never arrives on time.

   B Yes, he can be very _unreliable._

2 A She always thinks about other people.

   B Yes, she's the most .... person I know.

3 A Do you trust them?

   B Generally. I don't think they're .... people.

4 A These answers aren't right.

   B I agree. They're all ....

5 A She always wants everything now.

   B Yes, she's always been an .... child.

6 A This exercise is difficult.

   B Yes, I know! It's .... !

7 A Chips aren't very good for you!

   B Yes, I know they're .... , but I love them!

8 A He's 25, but he behaves like a teenager.

   B Yes, he's a bit ....

Reading

2 **a)** Read the article and write headings a)–d) in gaps 1–4.

a) The reasons we love soaps
b) ~~The origin of soaps~~
c) Popular soaps made in Spanish
d) Popular soaps made in English

Soap operas are one of the most popular types of television programme in the world. *Charlie Price* investigates the world of:

[1] *The origin of soaps*

In the United States, drama series started on the radio in the 1930s. The main audience was women, so many of the advertisements on the programmes were for soap. And at the time, western films were called 'Horse Operas'. Soon, people started calling the drama series 'Soap Operas'.

[2] _____

In the USA and the UK, soap operas can be on the radio or television for years. In the UK, *The Archers* is about people in a small village in England. The programme started over 55 years ago and it's still on the radio three times a week. Over four million people listen to each episode. *The Bold and the Beautiful* is a US television soap opera. It began in 1987 and is on television in almost 100 countries all over the world with an audience of over 300 million people!

[3] _____

In Latin America, TV soap operas are called *telenovelas*. A typical *telenovela* is on television five or six days a week for about three months. People watch Latin American *telenovelas* all over the world – even in countries like China, Poland and Russia. And the stars are often more famous than film stars. When the Mexican *telenovela* actress and singer Thalia, star of *Maria la del Barrio (Maria from the Neighbourhood)* went to the Philippines, the President met her at the airport!

[4] _____

A recent survey asked 300 people why they watched soaps. The most common answers were "They're relaxing", "They're part of my routine", "I like the characters". People also said that they <u>had to</u> find out what was happening in their favourite soap. When the Venezuelan *telenovela*, *Kassandra* was on television in Indonesia, the government became worried because some people were taking days off work to watch the programme!

b) Read the article again. Are these sentences true (T) or false (F)?

1 ☐ *T* Soaps first started in the USA.
2 ☐ *The Archers* is a soap opera on television.
3 ☐ The phrase 'Soap Operas' comes from the advertisements on the programmes.
4 ☐ *The Bold and the Beautiful* is popular all over the world.
5 ☐ Latin American *telenovelas* are usually on television for longer than British and American soaps.
6 ☐ *Kassandra* was a popular Indonesian soap.

6D Call me back

Leaving phone messages `RW6.1`

 1 Complete the phone calls with sentences a)–g).

a) No, thank you. I'll call back later. Goodbye.

b) I'm sorry. He's in a meeting at the moment. Can I take a message?

c) Yes, please. Can you ask her to phone me at the office?

d) ~~Hi Freddy. It's Val. Is Kate there?~~

e) Hello. This is Anthony Marsden here. Could I speak to Matthew Thomas, please?

f) OK. Bye.

g) No, she's out at the moment. Shall I tell her you called?

FREDDY	Hello?
VAL	¹ *Hi Freddy. It's Val. Is Kate there?*
FREDDY	² ....
VAL	³ ....
FREDDY	⁴ ....
VAL	Bye.

RECEPTIONIST	Hello, First for Food. Can I help you?
ANTHONY	⁵ ....
....
RECEPTIONIST	⁶ ....
....
ANTHONY	⁷ ....
....
RECEPTIONIST	Goodbye.

2 Read the messages and fill in the gaps.

> Shaun
> Dolores Pérez called this morning while you were out.
> Ring her tomorrow (Wednesday) at her office – 020 7289801.

DOLORES	Hi. Could I ¹ _speak_ _to_ _Shaun_ , please?
RECEPTIONIST	I'm sorry he's taken ² ....
.... off. Would you like to leave ³ .... ?
DOLORES	Yes, please. My name's Dolores Pérez. Could you ask him to ⁴ .... me .... ? He can ring me at ⁵ .... My number is 020 7289801.
RECEPTIONIST	Yes, of course.
DOLORES	Thanks. Goodbye.

> Mel – Ralf called. He's at home this afternoon. Call him.

RALF	Hi. It's Ralf here – Mel's husband. Is ⁶ .... , please?
RECEPTIONIST	Hold ⁷ .... , please. I'll put you through.
PERCY	Hello, Mel Parker's phone.
RALF	Percy? It's Ralf here. Where's Mel?
PERCY	She's in a meeting at the moment, Ralf. Shall ⁸ .... tell .... you called?
RALF	Yes. Can you ask her to call me ⁹ ....
.... afternoon.
PERCY	OK.
RALF	Thanks Percy. Bye!

 Reading and Writing Portfolio 6 p74

7A 50 places to go

Travel [V7.1]

1 Choose the correct words.

1 The best way to see London is on a bus (tour)/journey.

2 In this job you need to go on business *trips/travel* all over the world.

3 Mia has to *tour/travel* abroad a lot on business.

4 Did you have a good *journey/travel*?

5 We're going on a day *tour/trip* to Spain.

Present Continuous for future arrangements [G7.1]

2 a) Read the advertisement and the email. Then put the verbs in brackets in the Present Continuous.

b) Look at 1–6 in the email. Which verbs talk about the present? Which talk about the future?

1	_present_	4 ....
2	....	5 ....
3	....	6 ....

3 Look at Joe and Lina's plans for their holiday. Complete the sentences with the Present Continuous.

1 On Thursday evening _they're arriving in Cape Town._

2 On Friday evening ....

3 On Saturday ....

4 On Sunday evening ....

5 On Monday morning Joe ....

6 On Monday morning Lina ....

7 On Tuesday morning Joe ....

Fri 29 June	Visit Table Mountain
	Evening – go on boat tour of Table Bay
Sat 30 June	Go to Jamie's wedding
Sun 1 July	Drive to Camps Bay Beach
	Dinner with Jamie's parents
Mon 2 July	Start sailing course!
	Morning: Joe – have sailing lesson
	Lina – go to the beginner's class
Tues 3 July	Morning: Joe – go sailing to Robben Island
	Lina – go to the beginner's class
	Afternoon: go sailing

To: emma@capetownsailing.com
From: joe.pacelli@mymail.com
Subject: Sailing courses

Dear Emma,

I [1] _'m writing_ (write) about your advertisement for sailing courses in Cape Town.

My girlfriend and I [2] .... (travel) to Cape Town at the end of June for

a friend's wedding. We [3] .... (stay) for four weeks and we

[4] .... (look for) a one-week sailing course in July. At the moment, I

[5] .... (learn) to sail, but my girlfriend hasn't got any experience.

Please could you email me with prices and dates. I [6] .... (look forward)

to hearing from you.

Best wishes,

Joe Pacelli and Lina Waters

Do you want to learn to sail?

Learn everything you need to know in beautiful Cape Town, South Africa, in July or August. Courses for everyone!
emma@capetownsailing.com

a) Your friend, Cathy, is going on holiday. Write questions with these words.

1 Where / you / go ?

 Where are you going?

2 Who / you /go / with ?

 ....

3 When / you / leave ?

 ....

4 Who / take / you to the airport ?

 ....

5 Who / look after / the cat ?

 ....

6 Where / you / stay ?

 ....

7 What / you / plan / to see ?

 ....

8 When / you / come / back ?

 ....

b) Look at the picture and write Cathy's answers to the questions in **4a)**.

PASSENGER TICKET AND BAGGAGE CHECK
NAME: CATHY GRIGGS
FROM: LONDON TO CAIRO
DATE: 26TH JULY
RETURN: 9TH AUGUST

PASSENGER TICKET AND BAGGAGE CHECK
NAME: MIKE GRIGGS
FROM: LONDON TO CAIRO
DATE: 26TH JULY
RETURN: 9TH AUGUST

To do list
＊ Tell brother I've got tickets
＊ Ask Dad to take us to airport
＊ Ask neighbour to feed cat
＊ Book Hotel Altas ✓
＊ Buy book on Pyramids

1 I'm   *going to Cairo in Egypt.*

2 I'm ....

3 We're ....

4 ....

5 ....

6 ....

7 ....

8 ....

7B What are you taking?

Things we take on holiday V7.2

1 Do the puzzle.

	¹S	O	A	P
²		W		
³		I		
⁴		M		
⁵		M		
⁶		I		
⁷		N		
		G		
⁸		T		
⁹		R		
¹⁰		U		
¹¹		N		
¹²		K		
¹³		S		
¹⁴				

Quantifiers G7.2

2 Write *a* or *some* for the nouns in **1**.

1 *some soap*

2 *a towel*

3 ....

4 ....

5 ....

6 ....

7 ....

8 ....

9 ....

10 ....

11 ....

12 ....

13 ....

14 ....

3 Fill in the gaps in this conversation with *some* or *any*.

TIM	Right! We're nearly finished – shorts, T-shirts, sun cream …
CARRIE	Sun cream? I haven't got [1] _any_ sun cream.
TIM	That's OK. I've got [2] .... good sun cream. Soap, towels, …
CARRIE	Towels? The hotel will have [3] .... towels.
TIM	I suppose so. Toothpaste, film …
CARRIE	We don't need [4] .... film! It's a digital camera!
TIM	Oh, yes. Have you got [5] .... batteries?
CARRIE	Yes, I bought [6] .... new ones yesterday.
TIM	OK, chewing gum, toothpaste, …
CARRIE	You've already packed [7] .... toothpaste!
TIM	You're right! Have you got [8] .... sunglasses?
CARRIE	No, I haven't. I'm going to buy [9] .... at the airport.

Quantity phrases V7.3

4 Change the incorrect quantity phrases.

tube
1 a ~~bottle~~ of toothpaste
2 a bar of soap ✓
3 a roll of swimming trunks
4 a pair of sandals
5 a piece of shampoo
6 a tube of film
7 a bottle of tea
8 a piece of paper

5 Choose the correct words.

1 I don't have *many/(a lot of)* time to go on holiday.
2 There weren't *many/much* people in the hotel.
3 We only speak *a little/a bit* Spanish, but we'd like to learn more.
4 Nicola's got *a little/a few* euros, but not many.
5 Have you got *a bit of/a few* toothpaste? I forgot mine.
6 We haven't got *much/many* shampoo so I'll only use *a little/a few*.
7 Are you taking *lots of/much* clothes? I've only got a *few/a little* T-shirts.
8 The hotel didn't give me *much/many* information, but there aren't *much/many* beaches near here.

Possessive pronouns G7.3

6 Change the words in **bold**. Use *mine, yours, his, hers, its, ours* or *theirs*.

1 That's your towel not **my towel**.
   That's your towel not mine.

2 I didn't like the hotel. **The hotel's** rooms are really small.
   ----

3 A Is that Sue's sun cream?
   B Yes, it's **Sue's**.
   ----

4 That suitcase looks like **your suitcase**.
   ----

5 **Our house** is bigger than **their house**.
   ----

6 I haven't got a razor, but I'll use **John's**.

Review: spelling

7 S Correct these sentences.

information
1 Laurie's got some ~~informations~~ about bus tours.
2 That's not our towel, it's there's.
3 Who's sunglasses are these?
4 Have you got any chewin gum?
5 I need to buy a rasor tomorrow.
6 Have you packed the siutcase?
7 Can I borrow some teethpaste?
8 Can you give me that peice of paper?

Wish you were here

Reading

1 Read the article and fill in the gaps with these sentences.

a) Yes, the hotel has also got a private recording studio.
b) But you might need a rock star's salary.
c) ~~It has only got one suite!~~
d) Simon Page and his wife Susanah designed the hotel.
e) And if you want to do some exercise, there's a gym.

THE COOLEST HOTEL

IN THE WORLD?

If you like your privacy, then go to
mooghotel in Sydney, Australia,
says **Kristin Main**.

It's difficult to find a hotel more private than mooghotel. ¹ _It has only_
got one suite! Too small? Well, on the ground floor there is a living
room with a flat-screen television, a DVD player and a video games
machine. Upstairs there is a bedroom and a bathroom.
² .... Outside there's
a swimming pool and an outdoor cinema – all private, of course.
Go for a short walk and there's a marina – perfect for boat tours of
Sydney harbour.
   ³ .... They wanted
a hotel for people working in music and film to relax, and maybe
record a few songs. Record songs? ⁴ ....
....

   There isn't a reception at mooghotel, but there is a bar and restaurant,
moog wine + food. They offer over 100 different types of cocktail.
   Of course, you don't have to be a rock star to stay at mooghotel.
⁵ .... It costs around €600
a night, but that includes the use of the hotel's private Jaguar car, too!
Perfect for a quick trip to Bondi Beach.

Feeling musical?
mooghotel has got a recording studio!

2 **a)** Fill in the gaps with a
preposition if necessary.

1 You can go _for_ a drink near the
  hotel.

2 You can go .... swimming at
  the hotel.

3 You can go .... the hotel
  .... your family and friends.

4 You can go .... dinner in *moog*
  wine + food.

5 You can go .... a boat trip
  near the hotel.

b) Read the article again. Are the
sentences in **2a)** true (T) or
false (F)?

1 _T_   3 ....   5 ....

2 ....   4 ....

Expressions with *go*   V7.4

3 Fill in the gaps with the correct
form of *go* and if necessary, a
preposition.

ALAN   How about ¹ _going for_ a
        drink this evening? I want
        to get out of the house.

TAMSIN Good idea. We could
        ² .... that new bar in
        Devon Street.

ALAN   Can I invite my mum?

TAMSIN What? We ³ ....
        everywhere .... your
        mum! We ⁴ .... camping
        .... her last summer.
        We're ⁵ .... holiday with
        her next week.

ALAN   Tamsin! We're only ⁶ ....
        a short trip to Paris. It's not
        really a holiday.

7D I've got a problem

Complaints and requests RW7.1

1 Match the pictures to the complaints. You can use each picture more than once.

 room
 light
 lift
 food

 remote control
 bed
 air conditioning
 newspaper

1 It's broken. _light_ , ... , ... ,
.... , ...

2 It's too noisy. .... , ... ,
....

3 It isn't big enough. .... , ... ,
....

4 It hasn't arrived. .... , ...

5 It doesn't work. .... , ... ,
.... , ...

6 There's something wrong with it. .... ,
.... , ... , ...

2 Choose the best sentence for the situations.

1 There are no towels in your room. You say:
   a) I wonder if you could check my towels.
   b) Would you mind sending the manager, please?
   c) Could I have some more towels, please?

2 The air conditioning doesn't work in your room. You say:
   a) I wonder if you could check the air conditioning.
   b) Could you open a window, please?
   c) Could I open a window, please?

3 You ordered dinner in your room, but it hasn't arrived. You say:
   a) Bring my dinner!
   b) Could you check with room service?
   c) I'm sorry, but my dinner isn't hot enough.

4 The light doesn't work in your room. You say:
   a) I wonder if I could have another room, please.
   b) Would you mind sending someone to look at the light?
   c) My lights don't work!

3 a) Fill in the gaps with these words.

open	afraid	wrong	too
giving	send	speak	

1 The window doesn't _open_ in my room.

2 My bed is .... small.

3 Would you mind .... me another room?

4 I wonder if you could .... someone to check it.

5 I'm .... I've got a complaint.

6 Could I .... to the manager, please?

7 I think there's something .... with it.

b) Fill in the gaps with sentences from **3a)**.

DEAN Hello. I'm sorry, but I've got a bit of a problem. [1] _The window doesn't open in my room._

RECEPTIONIST Have you tried the air conditioning?

DEAN Yes, I have. [2] ....
It's really hot in the room.

RECEPTIONIST Oh, dear.

DEAN [3] ....
....

RECEPTIONIST Yes, of course.

MAGGIE Hello. [4] ....

RECEPTIONIST Oh, dear. What's the problem?

MAGGIE [5] .... It's a single
bed and I booked a double room.
[6] ....
....

RECEPTIONIST I'm very sorry madam, but we're fully booked this evening.

MAGGIE [7] ....

RECEPTIONIST Yes, of course. I'll call him now.

 Reading and Writing Portfolio 7 p76

8 Different cultures

Language Summary 8, Student's Book p134

Describing your home V8.1

1 Put sentences a)–i) in the correct order.

a) ☐ spacious. I live in a flat and it's on the top

b) ☐ morning. In fact sometimes I'd like air

c) ☐ got a large balcony. It's unusual for the

d) 1 I work at home so my home needs to be

e) ☐ in the day, but I don't mind. My flat has

f) ☐ floor. It's in a nice part of town and it's close

g) ☐ area. The balcony gets the sun in the

h) ☐ conditioning in my office!

i) ☐ to the town centre. It's quite noisy

Present Perfect for unfinished past with *for* and *since* G8.1

2 Write these words/phrases in the correct place in the table.

> five minutes   a few years   1986   ages
> this morning   I was young   ten days
> last month   a long time   two o'clock

for	since
1 *five minutes*	6
2	7
3	8
4	9
5	10

3 **a)** Read about Olive and Glen's home. Put the verbs in brackets in the Present Perfect.

Seven years ago we both retired. We wanted to move house, but we weren't sure where to go. I ¹ *'ve enjoyed* (enjoy) camping holidays since I was a child. And Glen ² _____ (love) driving since he bought his first car. So, we decided to buy a motor home. We tried living in the motor home in our garden at first – at weekends. Then three years ago we sold the house and we ³ _____ (live) in a motor home since then! Glen ⁴ _____ (have) a website about our life since January, 2003. Since we sold our house, we ⁵ _____ (stay) in over 200 cities, but we ⁶ _____ (never stay) in one city for more than a few weeks.

We ⁷ _____ (meet) some incredible people. Our present neighbour, Faith, ⁸ _____ (not move) her motor home for eight months. She only planned to stay in Flint for a few days!

b) Fill in the gaps with the Present Perfect and *for* or *since*.

1 They *'ve been* married *for* thirty years. (be)

2 They _____ (have) their second motor home _____ three years.

3 Glen _____ (have) a website _____ January 2003.

4 They _____ (know) Faith _____ two weeks.

5 Faith _____ (be) in Flint _____ eight months.

How long ... ? G8.2

4 **a)** Write questions in the Present Perfect or Past Simple.

1 How long ago / they / retire?

 How long ago did they retire?

2 How long / they / try living in the motor home at weekends for?

 ----

3 How long ago / they / sell their house?

 ----

4 How long / they / live / in a motor home?

 ----

5 How long / Glen / have / a website?

 ----

6 How long / their neighbour / live / in Flint?

 ----

b) Write answers for the questions in 4a).

1 _Seven years ago._   4 ----------------

2 ----------------   5 ----------------

3 ----------------   6 ----------------

5 Fill in the gaps with the verbs in brackets. Use the Present Perfect or Past Simple.

1 My mother _sent_ (send) me an email yesterday. She _'s had_ (have) a computer for six months and she loves it!

2 I _____ (not know) Eddie for long, but I really like him.

3 You _____ (work) here for 15 years now. Do you ever think about leaving?

4 Ollie and Abigail are a perfect couple! Where _____ they _____ (meet)?

5 I _____ (not live) in London for long. I really didn't like it.

6 Your boyfriend is very easy-going. _____ you _____ (be) together long?

7 We both _____ (study) French at university. Now we live in France.

8 Lizzie is a vegetarian. She _____ (not eat) meat or fish since she was 16.

Meet the parents

Going to dinner V8.2

1 **S** Write the words.

1 You are a *tuegs* at a dinner party. _guest_

2 The largest part of the meal is the *niam ruesco*. m_____ c_____

3 A formal way of greeting someone is to *kahse snahd*. s_____ h_____

4 The man who has a dinner party is the *tosh*. ------------

5 A sweet dish at the end of a meal is a *steerds*. ------------

6 An informal way of greeting is to *siks*. _____

7 The first part of a meal is the *rasttre*. _____

8 In some cultures it's rude to arrive *no mite* at dinner parties. o_____ t_____

should, shouldn't, must G8.3

2 Fill in the gaps with *should* and *shouldn't* and the verbs in brackets.

1 At dinner parties in England, you _should take_ some drinks or perhaps some flowers. You _shouldn't arrive_ without anything. (take, not arrive)

2 In many cultures, when you meet someone for the first time, you _____ hands. You _____ . (shake, not kiss)

3 In Hong Kong you _____ with your finger. You _____ your hand. (not point, use)

4 In Thailand you _____ your hat in Buddhist temples. Also you _____ shoes. Leave them outside the temple. (take off, not wear)

5 In many countries you _____ photos of people. You _____ them first. (not take, ask)

Make questions with these question words, *should I* and these verbs.

question words	verbs
~~What~~	give
How much	arrive
What time	exercise
Who	cook
Where	leave
How long	~~do~~

1 A _What should I do_ when I meet someone?

  B When you first meet someone, shake hands.

2 A _____ ?

  B Arrive between 7 and 7.30.

3 A _____

  the present to?

  B It's polite to give it to the hostess.

4 A _____

  the spaghetti for?

  B About eight minutes.

5 A _____

  my coat?

  B Put it behind the door.

6 A _____ ?

  B You should do about 20 minutes' exercise, three times a week.

 Fill in the gaps with *should* or *must*. Sometimes more than one answer is possible.

1 Harvey _must_ work harder this year or he will fail his exams.

2 Who _____ I invite to the party?

3 _____ I bring anything to the party?

4 Look at your hair! You _____ get a haircut before your interview!

5 This is important advice: you _____ carry your passport with you at all times.

6 I think you _____ take your umbrella. It might rain.

Infinitive of purpose

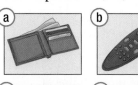 Match pictures a)–h) to sentences 1–8.

1 [d)] I use them to open doors.

2 [ ] I go there to get a suntan.

3 [ ] I use it to carry money and credit cards.

4 [ ] I go there to see films.

5 [ ] I use it to clean my teeth.

6 [ ] I went there to see the Eiffel Tower.

7 [ ] I use it to change the TV channel.

8 [ ] I wear them to see.

 Make sentences a) and b) the same. Use the infinitive of purpose in b).

1 a) I wanted to get a good view of London so I went on the London Eye.

  b) _I went on the London Eye to get a good view of London._

2 a) Jorge and I went to the language school because we wanted to learn a foreign language.

  b) _____

  _____

3 a) Clara needed to buy some new clothes so she went shopping.

  b) _____

  _____

4 a) I bought a computer because I wanted to use the Internet.

  b) _____

  _____

5 a) He wanted to watch the football so he stayed at home.

  b) _____

  _____

6 a) Silvia and Antonio needed to practise their English so they got jobs in England.

  b) _____

  _____

8C Cultural differences

Reading

1 Read the article and write headings 1–5 in the correct places A–E.

1 Eating and drinking
2 ~~Meetings and greetings~~
3 Making comparisons
4 Talking about money
5 Names and titles

Verb patterns **V8.4**

2 Fill in the gaps in the article with the correct form of the verbs in brackets.

3 Read the article again. What does the writer think? Are these sentences true (T) or false (F)?

1 | F | There are less than 200 different cultures in the world.

2 | | It's better not to talk about the subject of money.

3 | | The best way to greet people in different countries is to shake hands or kiss.

4 | | It's important to call people by their first name.

5 | | Food is always culturally important.

6 | | You will often prefer the way you do things at home.

Review: quantifiers

4 Write *a*, *an* or *some* for these nouns.

1 *some* bread
2 .... drink
3 .... email
4 .... information
5 .... advice
6 .... idea
7 .... vegetable
8 .... fruit
9 .... pair of trousers
10 .... air

Five cultural mistakes

There are almost 200 countries in the world, but there are even more cultures. Something simple that you do in your country might not ¹ _be_ (be) a good idea in another. Next time you decide ² _____ (go) abroad, this advice might ³ _____ (save) you from an embarrassing situation!

A *Meetings and greetings*

The safest thing to do is shake hands. But you always need ⁴ _____ (be) ready for different customs. In Japan, people bow. In Italy people often kiss. If I'm not sure, I wait and see what other people do. And don't wear gloves when you shake hands! Many cultures think it's rude.

B _____

When you meet someone, listen carefully to their name and any title – Mr, Mrs, Professor. If you didn't hear someone's name or title, then ask again. And don't forget ⁵ _____ (use) that title!

C _____

This is usually a difficult subject in any culture. You probably shouldn't ⁶ _____ (ask) someone what they earn. But in some cultures, it's common to discuss such things. So don't be surprised if someone asks you!

D _____

Food is important in almost all cultures. And many people believe their national food is the best in the world. So some things might be different – but they won't ⁷ _____ (kill) you! Try the local food and *always* say something nice about it.

E _____

Every country is different. And every culture does things differently. Yes, you probably prefer ⁸ _____ (do) things the way you normally do. But you're not at home now. So don't say "It's much cheaper *or* bigger *or* better at home."

43

8D What's Edinburgh like?

Adjectives to describe places V8.5

1 Do the puzzle.

```
 1        2
C R O W D E D
 3
     4
         5
 6
     8
 9

10
```

Across →

1 A There are a lot of people here!
  B Yes, it's always ...... on Fridays.
6 Many people think the English are
  ...... and cold, but I don't agree.
  Maybe it's because of the weather.
8 An adjective to describe food with
  very little flavour.
10 The weather in New Zealand is
  very .... It's sunny, then it rains
  and then it's sunny again!

Down ↓

2 The opposite of safe.
3 An adjective that means lots of
  tourists.
4 New York is a really ...... city.
  There is culture from all over the
  world there.
5 An adjective that means very cold.
7 Los Angeles is one of America's
  most ...... cities. The smoke from
  cars and factories can't escape.
9 A I need some more water.
  B Yes, the food is quite hot and
  ....

Asking about places RW8.1

2 a) Make questions with these words.

1 like / 's / What / Wellington ?   _What's Wellington like?_
2 Rio / like / 's / What ? _____
3 in Wellington / are / people / the / What / like ?

  _____

4 the weather / 's / in Osaka / What / like ?

  _____

5 in Rio / What / food / like / the / 's ?

  _____

6 the / like / Brazilians / are / What ?

  _____

b) Look at the table and answer the questions in **2a)**.

place	city	people	weather	food
Wellington, New Zealand	beautiful, but small	polite	good in summer, but very windy	excellent
Rio, Brazil	amazing	easy-going	always warm	delicious
Osaka, Japan	interesting	patient	freezing in winter	healthy

1 _It's beautiful, but small._   4 _____
2 _____   5 _____
3 _____   6 _____

Review

3 Correct the words in bold.

Japan

VIC   Have you been to **Japanese**, Owen?

OWEN   Yes, I **did**. I went to Osaka a few years ago.

VIC   What **does** it like?

OWEN   It's **too** interesting, but quite industrial.

VIC   Really. What **is** the people like?

OWEN   They're really patient. I don't
       speak **some** Japanese!

VIC   Me neither! Will you **going**
       back?

OWEN   Definitely. I plan to **going**
       to Tokyo this summer.

 Reading and Writing Portfolio 8 p78

Answer Key

1A Life stories

1 2 Where, d) 3 Who, c) 4 When, e) 5 Why, g) 6 How long, a) 7 How many, h) 8 How often, b)

2 2 did 3 are 4 are 5 are 6 did 7 are 8 do

3a) B What do you do in your free time? C How many countries did you visit last year? D What are you going to do tonight?

b) 2 'm looking 3 haven't got 4 plays 5 told 6 went 7 'm going to make 8 are going to do

4a) 2 Where did Annie go on holiday last year? 3 When is Annie's brother's birthday? 4 What does Sam do in his free time? 5 When do Heidi and Bob go to the cinema? 6 What is Annie going to do this evening? 7 How many countries did Sam visit last year? 8 Where is Annie going on holiday next year? 9 What are Heidi and Bob going to do this evening? 10 Where are Heidi and Bob going now?

b) 2 She went to Italy and Scotland. 3 It's tomorrow. 4 He works. 5 They often go on Fridays. 6 She is going to do her Spanish homework. 7 He visited four countries. 8 Next year she's going to Spain. 9 They're going to watch a programme on TV. 10 They're going to the cinema.

1B Super commuters

1 2 for herself 3 in London 4 with unemployed people 5 with young children, teenagers 6 in a department store 7 as a receptionist 8 for a newspaper, as a journalist

2a) 2 does Judy work 3 do Jess and Drew do 4 helps 5 works 6 works 7 hasn't got 8 likes

b) 2 *The Daily Times.* 3 They're teachers. 4 Ruth's job. 5 Ryan. 6 Michael. 7 Sally. 8 Stewart.

3 2 Who walks to work every morning? How often does Michael walk to work? 3 Which train goes to London? Where does this train go? 4 Who spends £200 a week on travel? How much does Jane spend a week on travel?

4 2 Who **missed the train**? 3 Where **does Ruth commute** to? 4 Which **book belongs to Jess**? 5 Who **is waiting to see me**?

5 2 Who has the longest journey? 3 Who gets up first? 4 What do you do, Ruby? 5 Who spends the most on travel? 6 Do you want to get jobs in London? 7 Who gets home first?

1C Time to relax

1a)

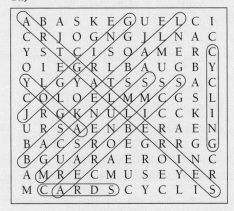

b) go: jogging, cycling
go to: art galleries, museums
do: aerobics, yoga
play: basketball, cards

2 2 James and Maria are **hardly ever** at home on Saturday evenings. They **normally** go to the theatre. 3 Are you **always** happy? You **never** stop smiling. 4 Do you **ever** do any exercise? I **occasionally** go running.

3a) 2 once a year 3 twice a day 4 two or three times a month 5 once every three months 6 every day

b) b) Theo uses the Internet seven times a week/every day. c) Theo reads a newspaper once a month. d) Theo goes to the gym two or three times a year. e) Theo goes on holiday once a year/ every year. g) Lily and Lionel never use the Internet. h) Lily and Lionel read a newspaper once a week. i) Lily and Lionel go to the gym three or four times a month. j) Lily and Lionel go on holiday two or three times a year.

1D Speed dating

1 2 So do I! 3 Neither do I. 4 Me too! 5 So did I! 6 Me neither. 7 Oh, I don't. 8 Neither can I.

2 2 So have I/Me too 3 Neither am I/Me neither 4 Oh, I did 5 Oh, I can 6 Neither have I/Me neither 7 So do I/Me too 8 So am I/Me too

2A Starting small

1a) 2 left 3 read 4 closed 5 wear 6 cried 7 stop 8 fell 9 think 10 made

b) 2–4 close, cry, stop 6–10 read, wear, fall, think, make

2a) 2 had 3 went 4 didn't finish 5 got 6 decided 7 wasn't 8 started 9 gave 10 opened 11 didn't … want 12 began 13 were 14 spent

b) 2 Who got a job selling ice-cream? 3 What happened in 1978? 4 When did they open their first shop? 5 What did they do on their first anniversary? 6 Why did they start the 'Ben & Jerry's Foundation'? 7 How many shops were there in 2004? 8 How much did we spend on Ben & Jerry's ice-cream in 2004?

3 2 Last 3 last 4 in 5 forties 6 ago 7 ago 8 yesterday

2B First meetings

1 2 were watching TV 3 was talking to a friend 4 was thinking about his girlfriend 5 was playing on her computer 6 were jogging in the park

2 2 was doing 3 saw 4 heard 5 was working 6 walked 7 were going 8 were talking

3 3 met 4 was travelling 5 wasn't feeling 6 were riding 7 thought 8 knew 9 visited 10 was going out 11 broke up 12 got 13 were staying 14 got

4a) 2 Where was she travelling when she met Shamil? 3 How was she feeling when she met him? 4 What were Shamil and Alexandra doing when they started talking? 5 Was she going out with anyone when she went back to Uzbekistan? 6 Where was her family staying when they got engaged?

b) 2 She was travelling through Uzbekistan. 3 She wasn't feeling very well. 4 They were riding their horses. 5 Yes, she was. 6 They were staying with Shamil.

Answer Key

5 2 **fall** in **love** with someone 3 **get** engaged to someone 4 **go** out **with** someone 5 **meet** someone for the first **time** 6 **break** up **with** someone

2C The 1001 Nights

1 The Lazy Man in Love: f), a), d) The Man and his Two Girlfriends: g), b), e)

2 3F At the start of the story Otiose didn't have a job. 4F Lothar was older than one of his girlfriends./ Lothar wasn't older than both his girlfriends. 5T 6T

3 2 until, d) 3 when, c) 4 because, e) 5 when/while, b) 6 so, a)

2D Small talk

1 2 do you know 3 What do you do? 4 Do you live 5 Are you a friend of 6 where did you meet 7 Didn't we meet 8 You're a teacher

2a) b) It was nice meeting you. See you again here probably. c) It was nice to see you again. Let's keep in touch. d) See you soon maybe. See you later then.

b) 2b) 3d) 4c)

3A Getting qualified

1a) 2c) 3e) 4b) 5f) 6a) 7i) 8k) 9l) 10g)/j) 11h) 12g)/j)

b) 2 opportunities for travel 3 sick pay 4 long holidays 5 friendly colleagues 6 a good salary

2 2 has to be 3 has to work 4 has to be 5 has to know 6 has to take

3 2 doesn't have to 3 have to 4 have to 5 didn't have to 6 have to 7 have to 8 didn't have to

4a) 2 Does … have to 3 Did … have to 4 Do … have to 5 Does … have to 6 Did … have to

b) 2 doesn't 3 did 4 don't 5 doesn't 6 did

3B Job-hunting

1a) 2d) 3j) 4e) 5c) 6h) 7g) 8i) 9k) 10a) 11l)

b) 2 be 3 earn 4 lose 5 get 6 write 7 look 8 fill 9 go 10 find

2a) 2 is 3 'm still learning 4 're watching 5 'm living 6 usually go 7 wants 8 are you crying

b) a)6 b)2, 7 c)4, 8 d)3, 5

3 2 're relaxing 3 drives, 's cycling/cycles, 's driving 4 's, 's raining 5 go, 're staying 6 lose, 'm winning/win, 'm losing

4 2 're reading 3 is 4 ask 5 Are … learning 6 'm studying 7 don't need 8 try 9 have 10 wants 11 's reading 12 arrive 13 'm waiting 14 read 15 need 16 helps

3C Strange jobs

1 2 writer 3 assistant 4 painter 5 musician 6 violinist 7 cleaner 8 director 9 cook 10 actor ↓ translator

2a) 2B 3V 4B 5N 6B

b) laugh, laugh advertisement/advert, advertise visit, visit cyclist, cycle paint, paint

3a) B5 C1 D3 E2

b) 2 decision 3 examination/exam 4 examiner 5 advertisement/advert 6 interviewer 7 discussed 8 excitement 9 swimmer

3D I'm really sorry!

1a) 2a) 3c) 4b)

b) b)2 c)4 d)3

2 2g) 3h) 4c) 5b) 6e) 7f) 8a)

3 1 'll 2 can't, 'll 3 have to, can't 4 couldn't, had to, 'll

4 2 I'm sorry, but I can't meet you later. I have to visit my parents. I'll see you at the weekend. 3 I'm sorry, but I couldn't go to the meeting yesterday. I had to go on a training course. I'll come to the next meeting. 4 I'm sorry, but I can't work on Saturday. I have to go to the doctor. I'll work late next week.

5 2 writing 3 swimmer 4 gallery 5 developed 6 shopping 7 opened 8 loses 9 opportunities 10 success

4A The silver screen

1 2 comedy 3 science-fiction film 4 musical 5 historical drama 6 war film 7 romantic comedy 8 western 9 horror film

2 1 were, been 2 cried, cried 3 did, done 4 went, gone or been 5 had, had 6 heard, heard 7 met, met 8 stopped, stopped 9 watched, watched 10 wrote, written

3 3 hasn't made 4 has made 5 has met 6 haven't met 7 have been 8 hasn't been

4 2 's learned/learnt 3 've … used 4 haven't tried 5 've … failed 6 've broken 7 have been 8 've driven

5 2 appeared 3 has acted 4 was 5 wrote 6 directed 7 won 8 have won 9 has done 10 has designed 11 has started

4B The rhythm of life

1 2 reggae 3 classical 4 pop 5 dance 6 jazz 7 blues 8 opera 9 rock'n'roll 10 rock ↓ traditional folk

2a) 2 Has Bob Dylan ever had a number one in the UK? 3 Have you ever bought a CD on the Internet? 4 Have you and Abby ever heard of the band Coldplay? 5 Have Cory and Amy ever sung karaoke? 6 Has your brother ever played in a band?

b) 2 he hasn't 3 I have 4 we haven't 5 they have 6 he hasn't

3 2a) 3c) 4c) 5a)

4 1 haven't, have, did … see, was 2 Have … been, have, haven't, hated, loved 3 Have … used, have, bought, did … buy, ordered, cost 4 Has … lost, has, lost, did … do, tried, couldn't, have … seen, haven't

4C TV or not TV?

1 2 The news 3 Turn off 4 reality TV 5 chat show 6 record 7 Documentaries 8 Soap operas

2 b) By 1955, 66% of American houses had their own television. c) In 1996, about 30 million people used the Internet. d) In 2005, there were over 650 million people online. e) There are at least 200 television channels on the Internet at the moment.

3a) 2 surprised 3 exciting 4 amazing 5 interesting 6 boring 7 tired

b) 2T 3F 4F 5T 6F

4D What do you think?

1 2 Do you agree with that 3 No, definitely not 4 Yes, maybe you're right 5 What do you think 6 Do you think 7 Yes, definitely 8 I'm not sure about that 9 What about you 10 I agree with

2a) 2C 3B 4D

b) 2–4: Do you agree with that? Do you think … ? What about you?
5–7: Yes, maybe you're right. Yes, definitely. I agree with …
8–10: I'm sorry I don't agree. No, definitely not. I'm not sure about that.

3 Students' answers

5A Man or machine?

1a) 2c) 3a) 4d) 5g) 6b) 7e)

b) 2 clean the carpets 3 feed the cats 4 look after my brother 5 build cars 6 take over the world 7 looks like me

2a) 2 Lots of people will work at home. 3 Cars will only use electricity. 4 Europe will have one government.

b) b) won't send c) won't be d) won't use

c) 2a) 3d) 4c)

3a) 2 won't buy, Will … buy 3 won't pass, Will … be able 4 won't be, will come

b) 2 will 3 won't 4 won't

4 2 I might study robotics at university. 3 Robots might become more intelligent than humans. 4 We might have computers in every room. 5 I might be able to understand maths. 6 My sister and I might be good friends.

5 2 can, 'll be able to 3 will … be able to 4 'll be able to 5 will be able to 6 can, 'll be able to

5B Never too old

1a) 2a) 3g) 4e) 5b) 6c) 7h) 8f)

b) 2 live 3 take 4 spend 5 do 6 learn 7 spend 8 get

2 2 I'm going to **retire** next month. 3 Are you going to **learn** anything new. 4 I don't know, but I' **m not** going to do anything difficult. 5 Is your wife **going to retire** ? 6 Yes, she **is** 7 And **what are you** going to do then? 8 I'm going to **spend** a lot more time out of the house!

3 2c) 3b) 4a)

4 2 spending 3 learn 4 have 5 having 6 live 7 retiring 8 be 9 retire 10 buying

5C Out of this world

1a) 1 Viking 1 and Viking 2 2 Mars Express 3 Beagle 2 4 Beagle 3

b) 2 to 3 to 4 with 5 to 6 on 7 to 8 about

c) 2 When, b) 3 Who, b) 4 Who, b) 5 What, a) 6 How, c)

5D It's for charity

1a) 2a) 3a) 4b) 5c)

b) 2 Great, thanks a lot. 3 Yes, that'd be great. 4 Yes, of course. 5 Yes, why not?

2a) 1 A group of comedians. 2 Millions of people wear red noses while they raise money for the charity. 3 Almost £250 million.

b) 2 Will you 3 I'll 4 Can I 5 don't 6 be

3 2 Why don't we ask Keiko? 3 Let's go to Poland. 4 Shall we go out this evening? 5 Could you give me a hand? 6 Can you make dinner? 7 Shall I buy some tickets? 8 Will you do the washing up?

6A Life with teenagers

1 **Across** 2 shy 5 ambitious 6 mature 7 polite 9 moody
Down 2 stubborn 3 considerate 4 honest 8 lazy

2 *-er* newer, older *-y → -i + -er* happier, moodier, funnier **double consonant + -er** hotter, wetter, bigger ***more* + adjective** more polite, more patient, more difficult **irregular** better, worse, further/ farther

3a) 2 worried 3 ambitious 4 more organised 5 selfish 6 stubborn 7 more impatient 8 more helpful 9 more interesting 10 polite

b) 1b) as organised as 2 as selfish as 3a) not as helpful as b) not as polite as

4 2 difficult as this one 3 more polite than ours 4 interested in football than my brother 5 shorter than her 6 more generous than I was a few years ago

6B Roles people play

1 2 nephew 3 grandmother 4 cousin 5 mother-in-law 6 stepson 7 ex-husband

2 2 relative 3 close friend 4 flatmate 5 neighbour 6 stepfather 7 brother-in-law 8 colleague

3a) 2c) 3b) 4a)

b) pretty: prettiest
polite, aggressive: a) most polite, most aggressive
bright, rich: d) brightest, richest
strange, nice: c) strangest, nicest

4 2 eldest 3 least 4 stressed 5 closest 6 lazy 7 brightest 8 least

5 2 the funniest 3 best 4 the most musical 5 the youngest 6 the thinnest 7 the busiest 8 happiest 9 the most stubborn 10 most organised.

6C Family Business

1 2 unselfish 3 dishonest 4 incorrect 5 impatient 6 impossible 7 unhealthy 8 immature

2a) 2d) 3c) 4a)

b) 2F 3T 4T 5F 6F

6D Call me back

1 2g) 3c) 4f) 5e) 6b) 7a)

2 2 the morning 3 a message 4 phone … tomorrow 5 my office 6 she there 7 the line 8 I … her 9 at home this

7A 50 places to go

1 2 trips 3 travel 4 journey 5 trip

2a) 2 are travelling 3 are staying 4 are looking for 5 am learning 6 'm looking forward

b) 2 future 3 future 4 present 5 present 6 present

3 2 they're going on a boat tour of Table Bay 3 they're going to Jamie's wedding 4 they're having dinner with Jamie's parents 5 's having sailing lesson 6 's going to the beginner's class 7 's going sailing to Robben Island

4a) 2 Who are you going with? 3 When are you leaving? 4 Who is taking you to the airport? 5 Who is looking after the cat? 6 Where are you staying? 7 What are you planning to see? 8 When are you coming back?

b) 2 I'm going with my brother, Mike. 3 We're leaving on 26th July. 4 My dad is taking us to the airport. 5 My neighbour is looking after the cat. 6 We're staying at the Hotel Atlas. 7 We're planning to see the Pyramids. 8 We're coming back on 9th August.

Answer Key

7B What are you taking?

1 2 towel 3 T-shirt 4 camera 5 shampoo
6 film 7 sandals 8 walking boots
9 suitcase 10 perfume 11 sun cream
12 sunglasses 13 make-up 14 shorts

2 3 a 4 a 5 some 6 a 7 some 8 some
9 a 10 some 11 some 12 some
13 some 14 some

3 2 some 3 some 4 any 5 any 6 some
7 some 8 any 9 some

4 3 pair 4 ✓ 5 bottle 6 roll 7 packet
8 ✓

5 2 many 3 a little 4 a few 5 a bit of
6 much, a little 7 lots of, a few
8 much, many

6 2 Its 3 hers 4 yours 5 Ours, theirs
6 his

7 2 That's not our towel, it's **theirs** .
3 **Whose** sunglasses are these?
4 Have you got any **chewing** gum?
5 I need to buy a **razor** tomorrow.
6 Have you packed the **suitcase** ?
7 Can I borrow some **toothpaste** ?
8 Can you give me a **piece** of paper?

7C Wish you were here

1 2e) 3d) 4a) 5b)

2a) 2 – 3 to, with 4 for 5 on

b) 2T 3F 4T 5T

3 2 go to 3 go, with 4 went, with
5 going on 6 going on

7D I've got a problem

1 1 light, lift, remote control, bed, air
conditioning 2 room, lift, air
conditioning 3 room, lift, bed
4 food, newspaper 5 light, lift,
remote control, air conditioning
6 light, lift, remote control, air
conditioning

2 2a) 3b) 4b)

3a) 2 too 3 giving 4 send 5 afraid
6 speak 7 wrong

b) 2 I think there's something wrong
with it. 3 I wonder if you could send
someone to check it. 4 I'm afraid I've
got a complaint. 5 My bed is too
small. 6 Would you mind giving me
another room? 7 Could I speak to
the manager, please?

8A Home sweet home

1 2a) 3f) 4i) 5e) 6c) 7g) 8b) 9h)

2 2–5 a few years, ages, ten days, a long
time 6–10 1986, this morning, I was
young, last month, two o'clock

3a) 2 has loved 3 've lived 4 has had
5 've stayed 6 've never stayed
7 've met 8 hasn't moved

b) 2 've had … for 3 has had … since
4 've known … for 5 has been … for

4a) 2 How long did they try living in the
motor home at weekends for? 3 How
long ago did they sell their house?
4 How long have they lived in a
motor home? 5 How long has Glen
had a website? 6 How long has their
neighbour lived in Flint?

b) 2 For three years. 3 Three years ago.
4 For three years. 5 Since January
2003. 6 For eight months.

5 2 haven't known 3 've worked 4 did
… meet 5 didn't live 6 Have … been
7 studied 8 hasn't eaten

8B Meet the parents

1 2 main course 3 shake hands 4 host
5 dessert 6 kiss 7 starter 8 on time

2 2 should shake, shouldn't kiss
3 shouldn't point, should use
4 should take off, shouldn't wear
5 shouldn't take, should ask

3 2 What time should I arrive? 3 Who
should I give 4 How long should I
cook 5 Where should I leave 6 How
much should I exercise?

4 2 should/must 3 Should/Must
4 must 5 must 6 should

5 2e) 3a) 4c) 5f) 6g) 7b) 8h)

6 2 Jorge and I went to the language
school to learn a foreign language.
3 Clara went shopping to buy some
new clothes. 4 I bought a computer
to use the Internet. 5 He stayed at
home to watch the football. 6 Silvia
and Antonio got jobs in England to
practise their English.

8C Cultural differences

1 B5 C4 D1 E3

2 2 to go 3 save 4 to be 5 to use 6 ask
7 kill 8 to do

3 2T 3F 4F 5T 6T

4 2 a 3 an 4 some 5 some
6 an 7 a 8 some 9 a 10 some

8D What's Edinburgh like?

1 **Across** 6 reserved 8 bland
10 changeable
Down 2 dangerous 3 touristy
4 cosmopolitan 5 freezing 7 polluted
9 spicy

2a) 2 What's Rio like?
3 What are the people like in
Wellington?
4 What's the weather like in Osaka?
5 What's the food like in Rio?
6 What are the Brazilians like?

b) 2 It's amazing. 3 They're polite. 4 It's
freezing in winter. 5 It's delicious.
6 They're easy-going.

3 Yes, I **have**. What **is** it like? It's **very**
interesting, but quite industrial.
What **are** the people like? I don't
speak **any** Japanese! Will you **go**
back? I plan to **go** to Tokyo this
summer.

9A Problems, problems

1a) 2a) 3c) 4f) 5d) 6b)

b) 2 overslept this morning 3 left my
wallet at home 4 missed the train
5 got … lost 6 got stuck in traffic

2 1 'll be 2 doesn't, 'll have 3 will, run
4 phone, won't 5 'll lose, don't 6 's,
'll leave

3 2a) If I see Caroline, I'll tell her you
called. 3b) If we go there again, we'll
stay at the same hotel. 4c) If he
doesn't study harder, he won't pass.
5f) If she's a vegetarian, I won't cook
any meat. 6e) If you write it in your
diary, you'll remember it.

4 2 If I miss the train, I'll have to drive.
3 If I have to drive, I'll get stuck in
traffic. 4 If I get stuck in traffic, I'll
be late for work again. 5 If I'm late
for work again, I'll lose my job. 6 If
I lose my job, I'll run out of money.

5 2 before 3 as soon as 4 when 5 as
soon as 6 after 7 before

6 2 I do my homework 3 he asks me to
marry him 4 she finishes work late
5 I won't stop learning English
6 You must go to bed

9B Sleepless nights

1 2f) 3b) 4a) 5h) 6e) 7d) 8g)

2 2 excited 3 upset 4 calm 5 worried
6 annoyed 7 guilty 8 sad

3 2 too much 3 too many 4 too many
5 too 6 too much, too 7 too many
8 too much

4 2 enough religion 3 enough time
4 long enough 5 often enough
6 enough money

5 2 warm enough 3 loud enough
4 enough money 5 exciting enough
6 enough salt 7 enough food
8 confident enough

6 2 They **haven't got enough** water.
3 They've **got too many** pairs of
sunglasses. 4 Warren **hasn't got
enough** money. 5 Hal **has got too
much** sun cream. 6 Warren **has got
too many** clothes. 7 They**'ve got
enough** bread.

9C In the neighbourhood

1 1 ✓

2 2 He thinks he's got quite a good
voice. 3 patient, considerate
4 Because Vaughan's radio is too loud
in the mornings. 5 He put the radio
on and turned the volume down.

3 2 get on with 3 goes on 4 give up
5 put up with 6 sat down 7 took off

9D Invitations

1a) 2 Are you free tonight? 3 What time
shall I come? 4 What are you doing
on Tuesday? 5 Are you doing
anything on Friday? 6 Would you
like to come to dinner on Saturday?

b) 2 What time shall I come?
3 What are you doing on Tuesday?
4 Would you like to come to dinner
on Saturday?
5 Are you free tonight?
6 Are you doing anything on Friday?

2 2 Would you like to 3 What time
shall we 4 How about 5 what are
you doing 6 Nothing special 7 Yes,
that'd be great 8 What about

10A Going, going, gone

1a) 2 is 3 are 4 are 5 am 6 are

b) 2 were 3 was 4 was 5 were 6 was

2 2 were bought 3 buys 4 bought,
were made 5 tried, was made
6 were written

3 2 met 3 got 4 moved 5 loved
6 wasn't taught 7 taught 8 got 9 was
paid 10 isn't run 11 works 12 join
13 are organised 14 use

4a) 2 published 3 grows 4 wrote
5 directed 6 painted 7 built 8 invent

b) 2 This book was first published by
Cambridge University Press in 2005.
3 Twenty percent of the world's sugar
is grown in Brazil.
4 The James Bond books were
written by Ian Fleming.
5 The Star Wars films were directed
by George Lucas.
6 The ceiling in the Sistine Chapel
was painted by Michelangelo.
7 Buckingham Palace was built by
John Sheffield, the Duke of
Buckingham.
8 Were online auctions invented
by Pierre Omidyar?

10B Changing trends

1 2c) 3e) 4a) 5b) 6f)

2 2 No**thing** 3 Every**one** 4 **no**where,
nothing 5 **Some**one 6 any**thing**,
something 7 any**where** 8 No **one**
9 Any**one** 10 **every**where

3 2 People didn't use to 3 People didn't
use to 4 People used to 5 People
didn't use to 6 People used to

4 2 didn't use to like 3 did ... use to
think 4 Did ... use to smoke 5 used
to live 6 didn't use to be 7 didn't use
to take 8 Did ... use to embarrass

5a) 1 Rosalie 2 Tricia and Julian
3 Sandra and Kyle

b) 2 What did they use to do? 3 Where
did Rosalie use to work? 4 Did
Rosalie use to be tired after work?
5 Where did Tricia and Julian use to
live? 6 Did they use to know their
neighbours?

c) 2 They used to go to the theatre or
meet friends for a drink. 3 She used
to work in Cambridge. 4 Yes, she
did. 5 They used to live in the city.
6 No, they didn't.

d) 2 Tricia and Julian 3 Rosalie 4 Tricia
and Julian 5 Sandra and Kyle
6 Rosalie

10C Fashion victims

1 2 – 3 a 4 – 5 an 6 – 7 an 8 a 9 The
10 a 11 a 12 the 13 the 14 –

2a) 2d) 3a) 4e) 5b)

b) 2T 3F 4F 5F 6T

10D Can I help you?

1 2 size 3 fitting 4 change, receipt,
5 sign 6 fit 7 pay 8 in

2 2 Have you got this in a smaller size?
3 How would you like to pay?
4 Check the amount and sign here,
please? 5 Have you got these
trousers in black, please? 6 Where's
the fitting room? 7 I like them, but
they don't fit. 8 Here's your change
and your receipt.

11A Guess what?

1a) get: lost, promoted
have: a problem, an operation
lose: a football match, your wallet
pass/fail: a driving test, a course

b) 1 21 years old 2 a train 3 out of
money

2 2 Arnie hasn't done the exam yet.
3 I've forgotten his name already.
4 I've just had an operation.
5 Robbie and I have just passed our
driving tests.
6 Have you found your keys yet?

3a) 2 have just had lunch 3 has just
arrived at work 4 's just finished a
report 5 's just found her keys
6 have just had a meeting 7 've just
been promoted

b) 2 Have Susie and Cath finished their
lunch yet? 3 Susie and Cath haven't
cleaned their desks yet. 4 Has Stan
told Edward about his promotion
yet? 5 Alicia hasn't printed her
reported yet. 6 Has Giles started
work yet?

4 2 Have ... had ... yet 3 's already
started 4 haven't heard ... yet 5 've
already read 6 've just bought

11B Murder mystery

1 2 **thief** 3 **rob** 4 **robbe**r 5 **murde**r
6 **murdere**r 7 **burgle** 8 **burgla**r

2 2 stolen 3 suspects 4 burglaries
5 shot 6 bullets 7 arrested 8 murder
9 victim 10 robbery 11 thief

3a) 2e) where 3c) that 4b) where
5d) that 6a) who

b) 2 where 3 which/that 4 which/that
5 where 6 who/that

Answer Key

4 2 They found a button **which/that** belonged to the murderer. 3 They closed the bar **where** the murder happened. 4 The bank **where** I work was robbed last week. 5 They found the things **which/that** were stolen in the burglary. 6 I failed an exam **which/that** I thought was easy. 7 We met the woman **who/that** is going to buy our house. 8 He got the cheque **which/that** I sent yesterday.

5 2 Someone has just stolen our car. 3 Have you read the newspaper yet? 4 She's been a suspect since the police found the body. 5 I haven't had an accident for a long time. 6 Everyone's already gone home. 7 Have you ever lost your keys? 8 We've never had an operation.

11C Here is today's news

1 1c) 2a) 3b)

2a) 2 verb 3 adjective 4 noun 5 noun 6 verb 7 verb

b) 2a) 3b) 4a) 5a) 6b) 7a)

3 2 Nothing. 3 It was robbed at the weekend. 4 Because they don't know what the robbers are going to do with 300 wedding dresses. 5 It had some spelling mistakes and it was written on the robber's CV. 6 They went to the address on the CV.

11D Did you?

1 2 's 3 was 4 've 5 does 6 have

2 2 Rod and Lin have lived here for ages. 3 I was working last night. 4 Cheryl does not work on Fridays. 5 Of course I've got enough time! 6 Tom's going to Poland on holiday.

3 2 Has he? 3 Didn't he? 4 Haven't you? 5 Can you?

4a) 2 Was he? 3 Don't you? 4 Did you? 5 Haven't you? 6 Did he? 7 Doesn't he? 8 Didn't she?

b) b)6 c)3 d)5 e)8 f)4 g)7 h)2

12A A year off

1 2 waste 3 spend, save 4 borrow, pay 5 lend 6 get 7 win, lose 8 spend, earn

2a) 2c) 3a) 4e) 5b)

b) 2 money can't buy you love. 3 the hardest things in the world to understand is tax! 4 I'm going to be a millionaire before I'm 30! 5 I'm working as hard as I can!

3 2 Present Continuous 3 would 4 could 5 is/are going to

4 2 said 3 tell 4 said 5 say 6 told 7 said 8 told

5a) 2 I'm never going to **get** promoted now! 3 I'm **working** really hard at the moment. 4 Every month I **spend** all my money on rent and food. 5 And I can't **save** anything. 6 We're going to **move** offices next month. 7 And my journey to work will **be** a lot longer. 8 I'm **leaving** next month.

b) 2 going to get promoted now 3 was working really hard at the moment 4 she spent all her money on rent and food 5 Joel that she couldn't save anything 6 were going to move offices next month 7 her journey to work would be a lot longer 8 Tia that he was leaving next month

12B Taking chances

1 2 insects 3 dye my hair 4 parachute jumps 5 karaoke machine 6 hypnotised 7 Tarantulas

2a) 2f) 3a) 4d) 5c) 6e)

b) 2T 3T 4F 5F 6T

3 2 would work, had 3 had, would give 4 would, told 5 would have, lost 6 would learn, spoke, listened 7 would live, didn't 8 could, would

4 2 If Edward wore a suit I would promote him to manager. 3 If Susie and Cath didn't talk so much, they would do a lot more work. 4 If Lenny didn't go out so late, he wouldn't be so tired. 5 If Alicia were more organised, she wouldn't lose everything. 6 If Giles lived nearer work, he wouldn't arrive late every day. 7 If I didn't worry so much, I would be a lot happier!

5 2 If the seats were comfortable, Chrissy would enjoy going to the cinema. Chrissy would enjoy going to the cinema if the seats were comfortable. 3 If we liked children's books, we would read Harry Potter. We would read Harry Potter if we liked children's books. 4 If my children lived near me, I would see them more often. I would see my children more often if they lived near me.

12C Men of magic

1 a)

2 2 Then 3 when 4 First 5 Next 6 After that 7 Then 8 Finally

3 2T 3F 4T 5F 6F 7T 8F

Reading and Writing Portfolio 1

1 d), e), g)

2 2T 3F 4F 5F 6T 7T 8F

3a) b)2 c)5 d)4 e)1 f)6 g)8 h)7

b) b)B c)E d)E e)E f)E

4 2B 3D 4G 5A 6H 7E 8C

5 2b) 3f) 4a) 5d) 6e)

Reading and Writing Portfolio 2

1 1a) 2b) 3a)

2 2 Because it was their anniversary – they started going out four years ago. 3 Ollie. 4 Because it said 'Will you marry me, Katy?'. 5 She wants Poppy to help her choose a wedding dress.

3b) It's <u>also</u> cheaper than I thought. And we can <u>also</u> go shopping. <u>What's more</u>, they were all smiling.

4b) <u>However</u>, that's the not the reason I'm writing … . We didn't drink it, <u>though</u>.

5 *However* and *though* contrast ideas in **two sentences**. We put *also* **after** the verb *be* and **before** other verbs. We put *however* at the **beginning** of a sentence and *though* at the **end**.

6 2 She sent me a text. I didn't reply, though. 3 He owns the restaurant. He's also a very good cook. 4 I'm not married. However, I've got a girlfriend. 5 We bought a new car last year. What's more, Mike got a new job. 6 I met a nice man last week. However, he's already going out with someone. 7 We got engaged last month. We're not going to get married until next year, though. 8 My parents met in 1975. They also got married that year.

Reading and Writing Portfolio 3

1 1 Jobs. 2 Ms Weston. 3 Assistant chef. 4 Simon Parks. 5 To summarise his phone conversation with Ms Weston.

2 3 pay 4 holiday 5 opportunities 6 promotion 7 two 8 hours 9 money

3 b) laurenweston@mailme.net c) 1988 d) Liverpool High School for Girls e) Le Moulin f) 2003 Liverpool Young Chef of the Year

4a) 1d) 2a) 3b) 4c)

b) Use bullet points (●) for lists:
preparation of meat, vegetables
Include important courses:
Northampton college, Hospitality and Catering course
Summarise your school examinations: 8 GCSEs including Mathematics, English and French
Include important work experience: Summer 2002 Le Moulin, Chantonnay, France
List other skills you have: Computers – word processing and spreadsheets

Reading and Writing Portfolio 4

1 b) *Win a date with Tad Hamilton!* c) *Minority Report* d) *Psycho*

2 3 Professor doesn't tell truth.

3 the year of the film: 1955
name of main characters: Mrs Wilberforce, Professor Marcus
other films made by the main actor: Star Wars
director: Alexander Mackendrick
the story: A musician rents a room in an old woman's house. When the woman discovers he is a bank robber, he has to kill her.
name of the reviewer: Melissa Parks

4 The bank robbers die and the old lady keeps the money they stole.

5a) 2R 3S 4R

b) 1 Present Simple 2 Present Perfect, Past Simple

c) the acting, the director, the place where the film happens, the story, other films by the actor or director

6 2 comes 3 hears 4 doesn't believe 5 listens 6 plays 7 meets 8 is 9 becomes 10 enjoyed 11 are 12 cried 13 liked

Reading and Writing Portfolio 5

1 2 Intensive English Plus 3 19 4 10 5 Bath 6 22 7 DS 8 DS 9 Language Links 10 Brighton 11 28 12 24 13 17 14 12

2 Paola: B Emre: A Daiki and Kiko: C

3 2 Sir/Madam 3 faithfully 4 Paola Conte

4a) 1 Dear Mrs Austin, 2 Dear John, 4 Yours sincerely, 5 Love, Kiko 7 Yours faithfully,

b) 1 would you be able to 2 I would be grateful if you could 3 with reference to 4 I am interested in 5 I would also like 6 further 7 I look forward to hearing from you soon.

Reading and Writing Portfolio 6

1 2A 3C 4E 5F 6B

2 2 Sam 3 Tara 4 Mum 5 Lucy 6 Clare's

4 3 I 4 You 5 I … the 6 I'll be 7 We/I … the 8 I

5 2 Mel Very important. Message on answerphone from police. They found car in Brook Road!
Adrian
3 Sarah If possible, can you call garage about car? Should be ready today. Thanks.
Chris
4 Jack Your flatmate rang. Got her keys? She can't find them and she can't leave house. Please ring her.
Lyn
5 Jan Going to cinema in Mason Road to see new Brad Pitt film. Please turn over. Meeting Rob for drink first. Want to come?
Macy

6 2a) 3c) 4f) 5b) 6e) 7d)

7 2 V. important. Message on answerphone from police. They found car in Brook Rd.! 3 If poss., can you call garage about car? Should be ready today. Thx. 4 Your flatmate rang. Got her keys? She can't find them & she can't leave house. Pls. ring her. 5 Going to cinema in Mason Rd. to see new Brad Pitt film. PTO. Meeting Rob for drink first. Want to come?

Reading and Writing Portfolio 7

1 1 a hotel 2 Brighton 3 friendly and helpful 4 Stratford-upon-Avon 5 talks and theatre tickets

2 2b) 3f) 4h) 5d) 7c) 8g)

3 1 Martin Griffin 2A

4a) a)2 b)3 c)1 d)4

5a) b) extremely c) about d) explanation e) would

6a) Dear Sir/Madam,
I recently had a week's holiday with *Shakespeare Tours* in Stratford. I'm writing because I was very, very unhappy with my holiday.
• It says that Stratford-upon-Avon is quiet. But our accommodation was opposite the bus station.
• The advertisement says that the teachers are qualified. They were university students.
• We went to the theatre three times. Only one of the plays was Shakespeare.
I said some things about the situation to the staff on the course, but they were as disorganised as the trips to the theatre!
I would like the money back for part of the holiday. My week with *Shakespeare Tours* was the worst experience I've ever had.
Please write to me soon.
Yours faithfully,
Corinne Blake

b) 2a) 3c) 4e) 5d)

Reading and Writing Portfolio 8

1 2e) 3a) 4b) 5c)

2 2F 3T 4F 5F 6F 7T 8F

3a) 2S 3D 4C 5C 6D 7S

4 2 In … with 3 to 4 from 5 to 6 to 7 from

5 2 Spanish food is quite unlike French food. 3 The weather here is like the weather at home. 4 The food is completely different from anything I've ever tasted. 5 Houses in the UK are usually much smaller compared with/to houses in the USA. 6 In comparison with British people, Italians usually dress better. 7 His new film is similar to his last one.

Answer Key

Reading and Writing Portfolio 9

1 a) Suzy b) Hilary c) Dave d) Sara

2 2e) 3a) 4f) 5d) 6b)

3a) 5

  b) b)4 c)5 d)3 e)1

4 1D 2B 3A 4C

5 3A 4A 5S 6S 7A 8S

  b) 2 the infinitive 3 verb+*ing* 4 the infinitive 5 *about* + noun 6 noun 7 *you* 8 the infinitive with *to*

6a) 2 I really think you should get another job.
  3 It might be a good idea to save some money.
  4 How about speaking to your boss.
  5 You could ask for a week off work.

  b) 2 It must be terrible to lose your passport on holiday.
  3 I completely understand your money problems.
  4 I'm sorry to hear about your brother.

Reading and Writing Portfolio 10

1a) For people's opinions on shopping on the Internet.

  b) 2F 3F 4A 5A 6F 7F 8A

2 against

3a) 1, 5, 8

4a) b)2, 3, 4 c)5

  c) 2 Firstly 3 My second point is 4 Finally 5 In my opinion

5 2 For instance 4 Therefore 6 However 8 I personally believe

6a) for

  b) 2 My first point is 3 For instance 4 Secondly 5 therefore 6 Finally 7 but 8 I personally believe

Reading and Writing Portfolio 11

1 2D 3C 4F 5B 6A

2 2F 3F 4F 5F 6T

3a) 1c) 2a) 3b)

  b) Past Simple, Past Continuous

4 2 crashed 3 broke into 4 were carrying 5 arrested 6 was waiting 7 was shot 8 were 9 found 10 was

5a) 1 A man. 2 About a robbery near the River Thames. 3 He rang his boss.

6 1b) 2a) 3c)

Reading and Writing Portfolio 12

1 a) Rupert b) Helen c) Paul

2 2 He tidied his room. 3 He's going to do some revision every month. 4 She's going to give up smoking and get fit. 5 She is going to see a hypnotist. 6 He's going to work less. 7 He's decided not to work at weekends.

3b) 2h) 3e) 4g) 5a) 6d) 7f) 8c)

4 8 She's going to be more organised about money. 9 She's paying her parents back. 10 She's going to plan her spending. 11 He's going to find a new job. 12 A couple of weeks ago he sent out his CV to a few companies. 13 He's going to stay in his job until he finds another one.

5 1 I'm a student **too** so I know how you feel. 2 I always spend more money **than** I earn. 3 **They're** very kind, but now I'm paying it back. 4 Then **if I have** enough money, I'll start saving. 5 **I'm** also going to plan my spending. 6 I **haven't found** any yet. 7 I **don't hate** the job I have at the moment. 8 But I need to find something with **better** opportunities for promotion. 9 I've spoken to my boss about it and she **understands** the way I feel. 10 A couple of weeks ago **I sent** out my CV ... 11 I think I **must stay** in my job ... 12 I haven't got **enough money** ...

9 Life isn't perfect

Language Summary 9, Student's Book p137

Problems, problems

Everyday problems `V9.1`

1 **a)** Match verbs/phrases 1–6 to words/phrases a)–f).

1	run	a)	lost
2	get	b)	this morning
3	miss	c)	the train
4	get stuck	d)	my wallet at home
5	leave	e)	out of time
6	oversleep	f)	in traffic

b) Complete the sentences with a phrase in 1a). Use the Past Simple.

1 I couldn't finish the report because I _ran out of time_ .

2 My alarm clock doesn't work and I ....

3 Can I pay you later? I .... this morning.

4 Sorry, I'm going to be late. I .... and the next one is at six o'clock.

5 Sorry! This map is terrible, I .... completely ....

6 The roads were really busy. I ....

First conditional `G9.1`

2 Choose the correct words.

1 If he (forgets)/will forget my birthday, I *am/'ll be* very angry.
2 If he *doesn't/won't* drive more slowly, he'*ll have/has* an accident.
3 What *will/does* we do if we *run/will run* out of money?
4 If I *phone/will phone* her now, she *won't/doesn't* worry.
5 You'*ll lose/lose* your keys if you *won't/don't* put them away.
6 If Bill *will be/'s* out, I *leave/'ll leave* a message.

3 Match phrases 1–6 to phrases a)–f). Then make sentences.

1	they not come	a)	tell her you called
2	I see Caroline	b)	stay at the same hotel
3	we go there again	c)	not pass
4	he not study harder	d)	not invite them again
5	she is a vegetarian	e)	remember it
6	you write it in your diary	f)	not cook any meat

1 _If they don't come, I won't invite them again._

2 ....

3 ....

4 ....

5 ....

6 ....

4 Write sentences with these phrases. Use the first conditional.

> I'm worried I'll oversleep tomorrow.

1 miss the train
If I oversleep tomorrow,
I'll miss the train.

2 have to drive
If I miss the train, I'll ....

3 get stuck in traffic
If I have to ....

4 be late for work again
If ....

5 lose my job
....

6 run out of money
....

Future time clauses with *when, as soon as, before, after, until* G9.2

 5 **Choose the correct words/phrases.**

1 He's not going to stop working *when*/*until* he's finished.
2 I'm going on holiday *before*/*as soon as* the conference.
3 We're going to buy a house *as soon as*/*until* we get married.
4 I'll do the washing up *when*/*until* this programme finishes.
5 I'm going to get a job *as soon as*/*until* I finish the course.
6 They're coming to my house *until*/*after* the football match.
7 You must do your homework *when*/*before* you go out.

 6 **Make sentences a) and b) the same. Complete the sentences in b).**

1 a) I'll ring him immediately after I get home.
   b) *I'll ring him as soon as I get home.*
2 a) I'm going to have dinner and then I'll do my homework.
   b) I'm going to have dinner before _____ .
3 a) I'm certain he will ask me to marry him. I'll say yes.
   b) When _____ , I'll say yes.
4 a) She might finish work late. She'll take a taxi.
   b) If _____ , she'll take a taxi.
5 a) I'll stop learning English when I can speak it well.
   b) _____ until I can speak it well.
6 a) You can watch the film. Then you must go to bed.
   b) _____ after the film.

 # Sleepless nights

Adjectives to describe feelings V9.2

 1 **Match the beginning of sentences 1–8 to endings a)–h).**

1 She's annoyed because her husband   *c)*
2 He's feeling depressed because his   _____
3 She felt confident when she   _____
4 I was really lonely when I   _____
5 He was really upset when   _____
6 They're tired because they   _____
7 They're bored because they   _____
8 I was very embarrassed when I   _____

a) first moved to London.
b) went into the exam.
c) ~~forgot their anniversary.~~
d) haven't got anything to do.
e) haven't had enough sleep.
f) new job is really boring.
g) ran out of money.
h) he broke up with his girlfriend.

 2 **Do the puzzle.**

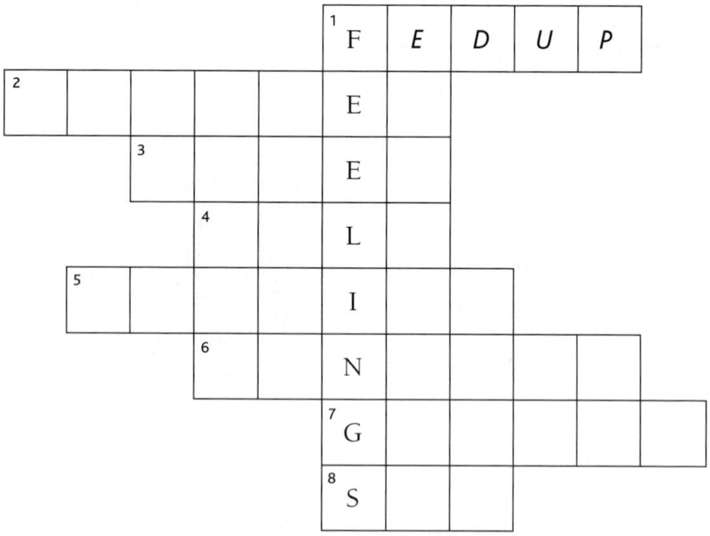

¹F	E	D	U	P	

(crossword grid with down answer FEELINGS)

1 Another word for a bit depressed.
2 Children get very _____ at Christmas.
3 When something bad happens, you feel _____ .
4 The opposite of stressed.
5 The adjective form of worry.
6 Another word for angry.
7 When you feel bad about something you did wrong.
8 Another word for unhappy.

too much, too many, (not) enough G9.3

3 Fill in the gaps with *too*, *too much* or *too many*.

1 When I met him I was __too__ nervous to talk.

2 I've drunk _____ coffee today.

3 I've had _____ sleepless nights recently.

4 I've heard that excuse _____ times before.

5 Conrad was _____ tired to come.

6 A What's London like?

　B There's _____ traffic in the city and it's _____ touristy in the summer.

7 There were _____ people in the queue.

8 You've always got _____ work!

4 Read the quotations. Choose the correct phrases.

I'm not ¹⟨young enough⟩/enough young to know everything.

(Oscar Wilde 1854–1900)

We have just ²enough religion/ religion enough to make us hate, but not enough to make us love one another.

(Jonathan Swift 1667–1745)

If you want creative workers, give them ³enough time/ time enough to play.

(John Cleese 1939–)

Life isn't ⁴enough long/ long enough for love and art.

(W. Somerset Maugham 1874–1965)

A lie told ⁵enough often/ often enough becomes the truth.

(Vladimir Lenin 1870–1924)

I have ⁶enough money/money enough to last me the rest of my life, until I buy something.

(Jackie Mason 1934–)

5 Complete the sentences with these words and *enough*.

| ~~time~~ money food salt |
| confident exciting loud warm |

1 There isn't __enough time__ to finish this.

2 I'm cold! It isn't _____ to sit outside.

3 Can you turn the TV up? It isn't _____ .

4 I haven't got _____ . Can I borrow some from you?

5 The film wasn't _____ for a thriller.

6 This is very bland. I don't think there is _____ .

7 Stay for dinner! There's _____ for everyone.

8 He's not _____ to talk to her.

6 Warren and Hal are going camping for the weekend. Look at the picture and fill in the gaps. Use the correct form of *have got* and (*not*) *enough*, *too much* or *too many*.

Warren *Hal*

1 They __'ve got enough__ tents.

2 They _____ water.

3 They _____ pairs of sunglasses.

4 Warren _____ money.

5 Hal _____ sun cream.

6 Warren _____ clothes.

7 They _____ bread.

9C In the neighbourhood

Reading

1 Read the article quickly. Tick the correct sentence.

1 ☐ Vaughan doesn't like Dominic.

2 ☐ Dominic is Vaughan's neighbour and friend.

3 ☐ Dominic and Vaughan play music in a band together.

2 Read the article again and answer these questions.

1 What does Dominic do to annoy his neighbour?

He plays his guitar and he does DIY.

2 What does Vaughan think of his neighbour's singing?

----

3 What two adjectives does Vaughan use to describe his personality?

----

4 Why did Dominic complain to Vaughan?

----

5 What did Vaughan do on the morning after he got the note?

Phrasal verbs V9.3

3 Change <u>underlined</u> phrases 1–7 in the article. Use the correct form of these phrasal verbs.

~~move in~~	go on	sit down
take off	give up	
get on with	put up with	

1 *moved in*   5 ----------------

2 ----------------   6 ----------------

3 ----------------   7 ----------------

4 ----------------

Neighbours. Everybody needs...

X ← → ⬇ ☐   http://whereveryouare.eblogs.net/r

blog (*n*) an online diary that is usually very personal

prev posts

comment

Wherever you are

A blog by Vaughan Simons

Neighbours. Everybody needs good neighbours.
Let me introduce you to Dominic.

Dominic is my neighbour. He lives in the flat downstairs. He ¹<u>started living in the flat</u> about two months ago. I've never seen him or spoken to him and I didn't know his name until last week. I'm a typical British neighbour – I don't need to ²<u>have a good relationship with</u> my neighbours.

Dominic plays the guitar. Well, actually he's learning to play the guitar. Every evening he comes home and plays the guitar. For an hour. Or maybe two. Sometimes it ³<u>continues</u> for the whole evening. And sometimes he sings at the same time. I can hear his voice clearly. In fact he's got quite a good voice. But he isn't a good guitarist.

Now, I'm a patient person. I *love* music. And Dominic is learning to play the guitar. I really can't ask him to ⁴<u>stop</u> playing his favourite instrument. So I ⁵<u>tolerate</u> his music, his guitar and his singing.

Dominic's other hobby is DIY. That means he builds things. His favourite time for DIY is on Saturday mornings. BANG BANG BANG. I don't know what Dominic is doing. But I know he likes doing it.

When I got home yesterday evening, I found a note. And that's how I know my neighbour's name is Dominic. It had three spelling mistakes, but it was polite. It said that he's working late every night at the moment. So, he often sleeps in the mornings. But unfortunately Dominic isn't getting enough sleep because my radio is too loud in the mornings.

I thought about what I should do. So I ⁶<u>sat on a chair</u>, ⁷<u>removed</u> my coat, and wrote a polite note to Dominic. I wrote about good neighbours, noise and being tolerant. But I didn't give it to him. This morning I got up, put the radio on and turned the volume down. I am too considerate, I know.

Nice to meet you, Dominic.

9D Invitations

Invitations and making arrangements RW9.1

1 **a)** Make questions with these words.

1 meet / we / Where / shall ?

   Where shall we meet?

2 you / tonight / Are / free ?

   ----

3 time / What / come / I / shall ?

   ----

4 Tuesday / you / on / What / doing / are ?

   ----

5 on / you / Are / anything / Friday / doing ?

   ----

6 you / Saturday / come / like / to / dinner / to / Would / on ?

   ----

b) Complete these conversations with the sentences in **1a).**

1 A *Where shall we meet?*

  B What about at your house?

2 A ---

  B How about between 8 and 8.30?

3 A ---

  B Nothing. Why?

4 A ---

  B Yes, that'd be great.

5 A ---

  B Yes. Why?

6 A ---

  B No, I don't think so. Why?

2 Complete the conversations with these phrases.

| ~~Are you doing anything~~   Would you like to |
| How about   What time shall we |

VIV   Hi, Doug. How are you?

DOUG   I'm fine. [1] *Are you doing anything* on Tuesday?

VIV   I don't think so. Why?

DOUG   [2] ------------------------------ go out for a meal?

VIV   Yes, I'd love to. [3] ------------------------ meet?

DOUG   [4] ------------------------------ seven? We can have a drink and then find a restaurant.

VIV   Yes, that's fine.

DOUG   Right. I'll see you in the bar next to the cinema. Bye!

| What about   what are you doing |
| Yes, that'd be great   Nothing special |

LAUREN   Joey, [5] ------------------------ on Wednesday?

JOEY   [6] ------------------------------ . Why?

LAUREN   We're going to see the new Spielberg film. Would you like to come?

JOEY   [7] ------------------------ . Where are you going to see it?

LAUREN   I'm not sure. I don't like the cinema on Park Street. It's too big.

JOEY   I know what you mean. [8] ------------------------ the one near the post office?

LAUREN   Yes. That's better. I'll tell the others.

 Reading and Writing Portfolio 9 p80

49

10 Shop till you drop

Language Summary 10, Student's Book p139

10A Going, going, gone

Present Simple passive; Past Simple passive G10.1

1 a) Fill in the gaps with *am*, *is* or *are*.

1 90% of the world's rice _is_ grown in Asia.

2 English _____ spoken in over 45 countries.

3 We _____ paid on the last day of the month.

4 Meetings _____ held every three weeks.

5 I _____ taught at home so I don't go to school.

6 A hundred watches _____ sold every hour on eBay.

b) Fill in the gaps with *was* or *were*.

1 That book _was_ written by an eighteen-year-old!

2 Your wallet and keys _____ found on the train.

3 That dress _____ worn by Madonna.

4 In 1995, eBay _____ called *AuctionWeb*.

5 I'm sorry, but they _____ sold yesterday.

6 The competition _____ won by a group of people from Liverpool.

2 Choose the correct words.

The most successful auction in the world
Fantastic **eBay** facts!

1 Today, eBay *uses*/(*is used*) by almost 100 million people.

2 $6.7 billion of cars *bought/were bought* in 2003.

3 Every 90 seconds someone *buys/is bought* a digital camera.

4 In 2001 the jeans company, Levis, *bought/were bought* a pair of jeans for $46,532. They *made/were made* in 1880!

5 In 2002 someone *tried/was tried* to sell the Earth! An offer of $10,000,000 *made/was made*, but the person didn't pay!

6 Between 1998 and 2003 over 100 books *wrote/were written* about eBay.

3 Read the article and put the verbs in brackets into the active or the passive. Use the Present Simple or Past Simple.

the man behind eBay

http://www.famouspeople.net/pomidyar.htm

The man behind eBay: Pierre Omidyar

On a public holiday in 1995, Pierre Omidyar [1] _created_ (create) the amazing online auction, eBay. But who is Pierre Omidyar and what does he do now? Pierre Omidyar's parents are from Iran. They [2] _____ (meet) in Paris in the 1960s. They [3] _____ (get) married and had a son, Pierre, in 1967. Six years later, they [4] _____ (move) to America. From a young age, Pierre [5] _____ (love) computers, but the subject [6] _____ (not teach) at his school. So Pierre [7] _____ (teach) himself on a small computer. Three years later he [8] _____ (get) his first job in computing – for the school library. He [9] _____ (pay) six dollars an hour! Now, more than 15 years later, Pierre is still chairman of eBay, but the company [10] _____ (not run) by him. Pierre now [11] _____ (work) with other websites like www.meetup.com. At Meetup people [12] _____ (join) others with the same interests. Then meetings [13] _____ (organise) in cities all over the world. Over three thousand people [14] _____ (use) the website to meet other English students!

Verbs often used in the passive V10.1

4 **a)** Fill in the gaps with the active form of these verbs. Use the Present Simple or Past Simple.

> manufacture invent write grow
> direct publish paint build

1 Every year Ford _manufactures_ six million cars.
2 Cambridge University Press first _____ this book in 2005.
3 Brazil _____ twenty percent of the world's sugar.
4 Ian Fleming _____ the James Bond books.
5 George Lucas _____ the Star Wars films.
6 Michelangelo _____ the ceiling in the Sistine Chapel.
7 John Sheffield, the Duke of Buckingham, _____ Buckingham Palace.
8 Did Pierre Omidyar _____ online auctions?

b) Write sentences 1–8 in **4a)** in the passive form.

1 _Every year 6 million vehicles are manufactured by Ford._
2 This book _____
3 Twenty percent _____
4 _____
5 _____
6 _____
7 _____
8 _____

10B Changing trends

anything, someone, no one, everywhere, etc. V10.2

1 Match phrases 1–6 to nouns a)–f).

1 something hot
2 somewhere cold
3 somewhere beautiful
4 someone amazing
5 something funny
6 someone rich

a) Nelson Mandela
b) a comedy
c) Iceland
d) fire
e) Cape Town, South Africa
f) Bill Gates

2 Fill in the gaps with *no-*, *some-*, *every-* and *-one*, *-thing*, *-where*.

1 This room is some_where_ I can relax. I love it.
2 A What are you doing tonight? B No_____ , why?
3 Every_____ is coming to the party. You should come, too!
4 It's boring here! There's _____where to go and _____thing to do.
5 _____one phoned for you earlier. But she didn't leave a message.
6 A I haven't got any_____ to wear.
  B I don't believe you. You must have _____thing.
7 I'm going to Warsaw next week. Do you know any_____ I can stay?
8 No_____ has seen him since last week. I think he must be on holiday.
9 Any_____ can do this. It's so easy!
10 I've looked _____where, but I can't find it.

used to G10.2

3 Fill in the gaps with *People used to* or *People didn't use to*.

1 _People used to_ have just one or two television channels.
2 _____ shop on the Internet.
3 _____ have credit cards.
4 _____ work six days a week.
5 _____ know smoking was unhealthy.
6 _____ believe the world was flat.

4 Fill in the gaps with the correct form of *used to* and the verbs in brackets.

1 I _used to believe_ (believe) in Father Christmas when I was young.

2 We _____ (not like) her, but she's changed a lot.

3 Why _____ you _____ (think) that?

4 _____ they _____ (smoke)?

5 Al _____ (live) here, but he doesn't any more.

6 Mobile phones _____ (not be) as cheap as they are now.

7 The journey _____ (not take) as long as it does now.

8 _____ your parents _____ (embarrass) you?

5 **a)** Read the article quickly and answer the questions.

1 Who now works at home? _____

2 Who now lives in the country? _____

3 Who has just had a baby? _____

Some decisions you make change your life. But how? We asked this question to five people.

Sandra and Kyle A year ago we went out at least three nights a week. We loved going to the theatre or meeting friends for a drink. Now, it's very different. Sometimes my parents look after Jack and we go out. But we usually stay in.

Rosalie Every day my journey to work was half an hour on the underground and then an hour to Cambridge on the train. And then back again in the evening! When I got home from work I just wanted to eat and go to bed. Now my office is only ten metres from my bed!

Tricia and Julian In our old house in the city, we didn't know anyone in our street. Now we know everyone. We've got children so we always need a babysitter if we want to go out. It was difficult to find anyone before.

b) Write questions with *used to*.

1 / Sandra and Kyle / go out a lot?
   Did Sandra and Kyle use to go out a lot?

2 What / they / do?
   What did _____

3 Where / Rosalie / work?
   _____

4 / Rosalie / be tired after work?
   _____

5 Where / Tricia and Julian / live?
   _____

6 / they / know their neighbours?
   _____

c) Answer the questions in **5b)**. Write short answers if possible.

1 _Yes, they did._

2 _____
   _____

3 _____

4 _____

5 _____

6 _____

d) Match these sentences to the people in **5a)**.

1 Life is more tiring now, but we're very happy.
   Sandra and Kyle

2 Now, if we're going out, we know at least five people we can ask.
   _____

3 I work a lot harder now – but I'm my own boss.
   _____

4 There aren't as many things to do here, but we feel much less stressed.
   _____

5 Now we sometimes rent a DVD, but it's difficult to watch the whole film.
   _____

6 My husband is much happier now because I'm not as tired.
   _____

10C Fashion victims

Use of articles: *a*, *an*, *the*, no article V10.3

1 Read the magazine article and fill in the gaps with *a*, *an*, *the* or no article (–).

Every week Trinny Woodall and Susannah Constantine give women advice about ¹ _–_ clothes on their TV programme *What Not to Wear*. Trinny started her career working in finance in ² _____ London. Susannah worked for fashion designers like John Galliano and then became ³ _____ journalist. In 1984 Trinny met ⁴ _____ Susannah and they had ⁵ _____ idea: they believed women needed ⁶ _____ honest advice about fashion and clothes. Every week they wrote ⁷ _____ article in ⁸ _____ national newspaper. ⁹ _____ articles became very popular and then they wrote ¹⁰ _____ book called *Ready 2 Dress*. After that, they made ¹¹ _____ TV programme called *What Not to Wear*.

Not everyone likes Trinny and Susannah. One person who was on ¹² _____ programme said "They are ¹³ _____ rudest people I've ever met". But Trinny and Susannah say they are just being ¹⁴ _____ honest!

Reading

2 a) Read the article. Match headings a)–e) to descriptions 1–5.

a) He doesn't try and he doesn't need to
b) Mr Average
c) ~~The suits~~
d) Bright shirt man
e) The successful fashion victim

b) Read the article again. What does the writer think? Are these sentences true (T) or false (F)?

1 [F] Italian men think more about clothes than British men.

2 [   ] Prince Charles looks good in a suit.

3 [   ] Shirts with big flowers are fashionable.

4 [   ] Type 3 thinks clothes are very important.

5 [   ] David Beckham looked good when he wore a skirt.

6 [   ] Most men in Britain dress boringly.

Clothes: The Five Types of British Man

Italian men are famous for their taste in fashion. British men are a little different! Here's our quick guide to the five types of British man.

1 *The suits*

Most men look good in a suit if it isn't too bright. Prince Charles is a great example of this. His suits aren't fashionable, but he's got a 'classic' look.

2 _____

His clothes don't fit and they were fashionable about ten years ago. He's probably wearing a light shirt, perhaps yellow or orange and probably with big flowers. And he's got an earring. So he must be cool!

3 _____

He doesn't look like he ever thinks about clothes. He looks like he got dressed in about ten seconds. But he still looks fantastic and very stylish. Ewan McGregor is a perfect example.

4 _____

The most unusual type of British man. They're brave and they take chances with their clothes. They've got their own style and they love to experiment with clothes. They are *usually* successful, but remember David Beckham and the skirt?

5 _____

The opposite of type 4, this man's clothes are BORING. This is the largest group of men in the UK. They wear jeans, T-shirts and if it's cold, a jumper. Oh, yes – don't forget the trainers!

10D Can I help you?

Shopping V10.4

1 Complete the sentences in each picture with these words.

| ~~try on~~ | size | pay | receipt | in |
| fitting | sign | change | fit | |

¹Can I _try_ this _on_ ?

²Have you got this in a smaller _____ ?

³Where's the _____ room?

⁴Here's your _____ and your _____ .

⁵Check the amount and _____ here, please.

⁶I like them, but they don't _____ .

⁷How would you like to _____ ?

⁸Have you got these trousers _____ black, please?

In a shop RW10.1

2 Complete the conversations with the sentences in **1**.

1

EILEEN   ¹ *Can I try this on, please?*

ASSISTANT   Yes, of course.

EILEEN   ² _____

ASSISTANT   Yes, I think so. Here you are.

EILEEN   Great. I'll just try it on.

ASSISTANT   OK.

EILEEN   It's perfect. I'll take it.

ASSISTANT   Fine. ³ _____

EILEEN   With a credit card, please.

ASSISTANT   OK. ⁴ _____

EILEEN   Thanks.

ASSISTANT   You're welcome. And here's your receipt.

2

KIRK   ⁵ _____

ASSISTANT   I'll have a look. Yes, here's a pair of black ones.

KIRK   Great, thanks. ⁶ _____

ASSISTANT   It's over there.

KIRK   Thanks.

KIRK   Hmm. ⁷ _____

ASSISTANT   No, they're a bit small. I'll have a look for a larger size.

KIRK   Thanks.

ASSISTANT   That's £39.99, please.

KIRK   Here you are.

ASSISTANT   Thanks. ⁸ _____

KIRK   Thanks. A penny!

 Reading and Writing Portfolio 10 p82

Language Summary 11, Student's Book p141

11A Guess what?

Verb-noun collocations (3) **V11.1**

1 a) Fill in the gaps with these words/phrases. There are three extra words/phrases.

a train	lost	out of money
a problem	a football match
an operation	your wallet
a driving test	a course
21 years old	promoted

get

_____ _____

sacked

have

_____ _____

an accident

lose

_____ _____

your keys

pass/fail

_____ _____

an exam

b) Match the extra words/phrases in **1a)** to these verbs.

1 be _____

2 miss _____

3 run _____

Present Perfect for giving news with *just, yet* and *already* **G11.1**

2 Make sentences with these words.

1 you / sent / just / I've / email / an ! *I've just sent you an email!*

2 yet / exam / hasn't / the / done / Arnie .

_____

3 forgotten / name / already / I've / his .

_____

4 had / operation / just / I've / an .

_____

5 driving tests / passed / Robbie and I / just / have / our .

_____

6 yet / you / your / found / Have / keys ?

_____

3 a) Look at the picture. Complete the sentences with these phrases. Use the Present Perfect and *just*.

go shopping
find her keys
arrive at work
have a meeting
get promoted
have lunch
finish a report

1 Lenny *'s just been shopping.*

2 Susie and Cath _____

3 Giles _____ .

4 Alicia _____ .

5 Ella _____ .

6 Stan and Edward _____ .

7 EDWARD I _____ .

b) Write negative sentences and questions with these words and *yet*.

1 Lenny / not turn on / his computer / .

   Lenny hasn't turned on his computer yet.

2 / Susie and Cath / finish / their lunch / ?

   ....

   ....

3 Susie and Cath / not clean / their desks / .

   ....

   ....

4 / Stan / tell / Edward about his promotion / ?

   ....

   ....

5 Alicia / not print / her report / .

   ....

   ....

6 / Giles / start / work / ?

   ....

   ....

 4 Fill in the gaps with these verbs. Use the Present Perfect and *just*, *yet* or *already*.

~~leave~~ start have read buy hear

1 A Can I speak to Evelyn, please?

   B I'm sorry, but she *'s already left* . (already)

2 A They got married a few years ago.

   B .... they .... any children

      .... ? (yet)

3 A Do we have to run?

   B Yes! The film .... (already)

4 A Do you like this group?

   B Yes, but I .... their new CD

      .... (yet)

5 A Do you like the book I gave you?

   B Yes, but unfortunately I ....

      it. (already)

6 A Have you got any coffee?

   B Yes, I .... some. (just)

11B **Murder mystery**

Crime V11.2 V11.3

 1 Complete the words in the table.

crime	verb	criminal
theft	1 st<u>e</u> <u>a</u>l	2 th_ _f
robbery	3 r_ _	4 r_ _ _ _r
murder	5 m_ _ _ _r	6 m_ _ _ _ _ _r
burglary	7 b_ _ _ _e	8 b_ _ _ _ _r

2 Fill in the gaps in the articles with these words/phrases.

~~broken into~~ murder shot thief stolen bullets arrested victim robbery burglaries suspects

Four houses in Dover Street were [1] *broken into* yesterday. Jewellery, televisions and DVD players were [2] .... The police are interviewing two [3] .... in connection with the [4] ....

A man died yesterday after he was [5] .... in a bar in the Newton area of Boston. Doctors found three [6] .... in his body. A woman was [7] .... last night in connection with the [8] ....

Kevin Spacey, the Hollywood actor, was the [9] .... of a [10] .... in a park in South London last night. Spacey was walking his dog early in the morning when a young man stopped him. He asked to use Spacey's mobile phone. When Spacey gave him the phone, the young [11] .... ran away.

Relative clauses with *who*, *which*, *that* and *where* `G11.2`

 a) Read the articles in **2** again. Match beginnings 1–6 to endings a)–f). Choose the correct relative pronoun.

①  ②  ③

④  ⑤  ⑥

1 This is the phone
2 This is the park
3 These are the houses
4 This is the bar
5 These are the things
6 This is the woman

a) *who/which* murdered the man.
b) *which/where* the man was murdered.
c) *that/where* were broken into.
d) *where/that* were stolen.
e) *where/which* Spacey was robbed.
f) *that/who* was stolen.

b) Complete the sentences with *who*, *which*, *that* or *where*. Sometimes more than one answer is possible.

1 The man _who/that_ was robbed is an actor.
2 The park _____ Kevin Spacey was robbed is in South London.
3 The houses _____ were burgled were in Dover Street.
4 The things _____ were stolen included televisions and DVD players.
5 The bar _____ the man was shot is in the Newton area.
6 The man _____ was shot died in hospital.

④ Write the correct relative pronoun in the sentences. Sometimes more than one answer is possible.

              who
1 The police arrested a young man‸lives in my street.
2 They found a button belonged to the murderer.
3 They closed the bar the murder happened.
4 The bank I work was robbed last week.
5 They found the things were stolen in the burglary.
6 I failed an exam I thought was easy.
7 We met the woman is going to buy our house.
8 He got the cheque I sent yesterday.

Review: Present Perfect

⑤ Write sentences in the Present Perfect. Use the words in brackets.

1 The police / not arrest / anyone for Jack's murder / . (yet)
   The police haven't arrested anyone for Jack's murder yet.

2 Ring the police! Someone / steal / our car. (just)
   _____

3 / you / read / the newspaper / ? (yet) There's an article about Jack's murder.
   _____

4 She / be / a suspect / the police found the body. (since)
   _____

5 I / not have / an accident / a long time. (for)
   _____

6 You're too late. Everyone / go / home! (already)
   _____

7 / you / lose / your keys? (ever)
   _____

8 We / have / an operation. (never)
   _____

Here is today's news

Reading

1 Write headings a)–c) in the correct places 1–3.

a) **Thief steals wedding day dreams**

b) **ROBBER ALMOST FINDS JOB**

c) **WOMAN GETS PARKING TICKET IN TRAFFIC JAM**

1 _____

Last week Hedda Ibsen was stuck in traffic in the middle of Oslo, Norway. She was sitting in her car, when a parking attendant gave her a ticket and a ¹**fine** for £50. Hedda, 32, couldn't believe it. She argued with the parking attendant, but he ²**refused** to take the ticket back. Hedda had to go to court to explain the situation. The court agreed with Hedda and told the traffic department to pay her £300.

"I'm really ³**glad** I won," she said on Friday.

2 _____

$230,000 of wedding dresses, were stolen from a ⁴**store** in Vancouver, Canada, last weekend. The robbery was discovered on Monday morning at *Wedding World*. Police officer Den Kerry said "This is a weird robbery. What are they going to do with 300 wedding dresses? You can't sell them at a market. Some of the stolen dresses were for weddings next week, so there will be a few unhappy ⁵**brides**."

3 _____

A man who robbed a bank in Texas, USA, was arrested yesterday after he left behind his CV! The man walked into the bank and ⁶**handed** the assistant a note. It said: *Don't say anythang or I'll shot you.* "I thought it was a joke," laughed Ivy Harris, the assistant. "I wanted to show him the spelling mistakes."

Ivy gave the man the money. When he left, she realised the note was written on the back of someone's CV. The police went to the address on the CV and found the robber, Justin Hewitt. He was ⁷**counting** the stolen money. The first thing he said was "It's more than I thought!"

Guessing meaning from context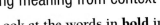

2 **a)** Look at the words in **bold** in the article. Are they nouns, verbs or adjectives?

1 fine ___*noun*___ 5 brides _____

2 refused _____ 6 handed _____

3 glad _____ 7 counting _____

4 store _____

b) Choose the correct meanings of the words in **2a)**.

1 fine
a) money that is paid as punishment
b) a cheque

2 refuse
a) say you will not do something
b) agree to do something

3 glad
a) sad b) happy

4 store
a) shop b) house

5 brides
a) women who are getting married soon
b) men who are getting married soon

6 handed
a) sent b) gave

7 counting
a) finding the total of b) spending

3 Answer the questions.

1 How much was the fine?

___£50___

2 How much did Hedda pay the parking attendant?

_____

3 When was the store robbed?

_____

4 Why did the police office think the wedding dress robbery was unusual?

_____

5 What was funny about the note Ivy was handed?

_____

6 How did the police find Justin Hewitt?

_____

11D Did you?

Review: auxiliary verbs

1 Fill in the gaps with the correct form of the auxiliary verbs *do, be* or *have*.

1 Hank _has_ phoned you twice today.

2 Tom _____ going to Poland on holiday.

3 I _____ working last night.

4 Of course I _____ got enough time!

5 Cheryl _____ not work on Fridays.

6 Rod and Lin _____ lived here for ages.

Echo questions   RW11.1

2 Complete these short conversations with the sentences in **1**.

1 A _Hank has phoned you twice today._

  B Has he?

2 A _____

  _____

  B Have they?

3 A _____

  _____

  _____

  B Were you?

4 A _____

  _____

  _____

  B Doesn't she?

5 A _____

  _____

  _____

  B Have you?

6 A _____

  _____

  _____

  B Is he?

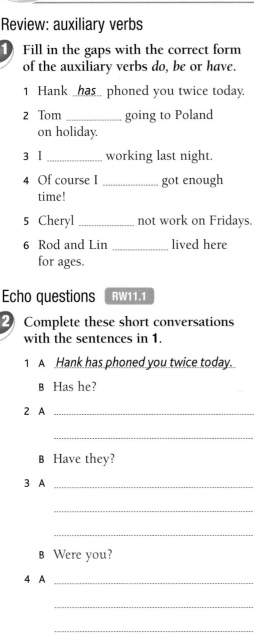

3 Choose the correct echo questions.

BOB Where's Adrian?

DENISE He's on holiday.

BOB ¹*Does he/Is he?/Has he?*

DENISE Yes, he's been on holiday three times this year.

BOB ²*Has he?/Have he?/Had he?* Lucky him!

DENISE Lucky? He's lazy! He didn't finish the sales report before he went.

BOB ³*Doesn't he?/Didn't he?/Did he?* Who is going to finish it?

DENISE I don't know. I haven't got enough time.

BOB ⁴*Didn't you?/Have you?/Haven't you?* Oh, dear. Maybe I can …

DENISE ⁵*Can you?/Can't you?/Can he?* You're so helpful. Thanks so much.

4 **a)** Write echo questions for these sentences.

1 A The police have arrested two people in our street.

  B _Have they?_ What for?

2 A Malcolm was on a quiz show last night.

  B _____? Which one?

3 A I don't like coffee.

  B _____? What about tea?

4 A I used to live abroad.

  B _____? Where?

5 A We haven't seen him for ages.

  B _____? When was the last time?

6 A Norman got promoted last week.

  B _____? What's his new job?

7 A Sorry. Gavin doesn't work here anymore.

  B _____? Where does he work now?

8 A Libby didn't turn up this morning.

  B _____? What happened to her?

b) Match answers a)–h) to the echo questions in **4a)**.

a) [1] Burglary, I think.

b) [ ] He's now my manager!

c) [ ] Yes, but only with lemon.

d) [ ] About four months ago, I think.

e) [ ] I'm not sure, but I think she overslept.

f) [ ] Lots of countries – Brazil, Portugal, Mozambique.

g) [ ] He got a job in London.

h) [ ] It was called *Millionaire*.

 Reading and Writing Portfolio 11 p84

12 Achieving your goals

Language Summary 12, Student's Book p143

A year off

Money

1 Choose the correct words.

MONEY MATTERS

Some **advice** from our **money experts**

1 Not everything that (costs)/buys a lot of money is good.

2 Don't *waste/save* money on things you don't need!

3 Don't *spend/lose* all your money every month. Try to *lend/save* a little money when you can.

4 If you need to *borrow/lend* money, think about how and when you will *pay/buy* it back.

5 Money and friendship don't mix. Don't *borrow/lend* a lot of money to friends.

6 When you take money out of the bank, only *get/borrow* the money you need.

7 If you want to *earn/win* money, you must be prepared to *lose/save* it!

8 This is simple, but very important: you mustn't *spend/cost* more money than you *earn/win* !

Reported speech

2 a) Match beginnings of sentences 1–5 to endings a)–e).

1 When I was young my father told me
2 The Beatles said that
3 Albert Einstein was very intelligent, but he said that
4 His email said that
5 I told them that

a) the hardest thing in the world to understand was tax!
b) I was working as hard as I could!
c) money couldn't buy you love.
d) money would be important one day.
e) he was going to be a millionaire before he was 30!

b) Write the sentences in **2a)** in direct speech.

1 My father told me "*Money will be important one day.*"

2 The Beatles said " _____

_____ ."

3 Albert Einstein was very intelligent, but he said " _____

_____ .

4 His email said " _____

_____ ."

5 I told them " _____

_____ ."

3 Complete the table with Present Continuous, *is/are going to*, Past Simple, *could* and *would*.

verb form in direct speech	verb form in reported speech
Present Simple	1 *Past Simple*
2	Past Continuous
will	3
can	4
5	was/were going to

4 Choose the correct words.

1 I *said/(told)* my boss that I didn't earn enough.
2 Everyone *said/told* he borrowed a lot of money.
3 Did I *say/tell* you I was moving abroad?
4 Mark *said/told* that he never wasted anything.
5 How much did you *say/tell* it cost?
6 No one *said/told* me that I had to pay the money back!
7 You *said/told* that you could lend me the money.
8 Frances *said/told* her she was going to save her money for her holiday.

5 **a)** Joel is talking to his colleague, Tia. Fill in the gaps in the conversation with the correct form of the verbs in brackets.

JOEL   Are you OK, Tia? You don't look very happy.

TIA   [1]I __'m__ (be) a bit fed up. Ellie got promoted last week. [2]I'm never going to _____ (get) promoted now!

JOEL   Ellie got promoted? I don't believe it!

TIA   Neither do I. [3]I'm _____ (work) really hard at the moment.

JOEL   Yes, me too. It's not fair, is it?

TIA   [4]Every month I _____ (spend) all my money on rent and food. [5]And I can't _____ (save) anything.

JOEL   Yes, it's really expensive here.

TIA   [6]We're going to _____ (move) offices next month. [7]And my journey to work will _____ (be) a lot longer. Why are you so happy?

JOEL   Well, I haven't told you yet. [8]I'm _____ (leave) next month.

TIA   Leaving? Now I won't have anyone to talk to!

b) Write sentences 1–8 in **5a)** in reported speech.

1 Tia said that __she was a bit fed up.__

2 She told Joel that she was never _____ _____ .

3 She said that she _____ _____ .

4 She said that every month _____ _____ .

5 She told _____ _____ .

6 She said that they _____ _____ .

7 She told Joel that _____ _____ .

8 Joel told _____ _____ .

12B Taking chances

Unusual activities V12.2

1 Fill in the gaps with the correct form of these words.

> ~~glove~~   dye my/your hair   karaoke machine
> parachute jump   hypnotise   tarantula   insect

1 Have you seen my other __glove__ ? I can only find one.

2 Many people think spiders are _____ , but they aren't.

3 I always wanted to _____ , but now I'm bald!

4 Dawn's done three _____ for charity.

5 Derek's got a _____ and he's good at singing.

6 I was _____ once – I don't remember a thing about it!

7 _____ aren't dangerous to humans and can be trained as pets.

Second conditional G12.2

2 **a)** Match beginnings of sentences 1–6 to endings a)–f).

1 If Erin owed Hal any money, __b)__

2 If Don asked me to marry him, _____

3 If I didn't earn a lot of money, _____

4 If Connor dyed his hair, _____

5 If Debbie left the company, _____

6 If Mo didn't work so hard, _____

a) I wouldn't work so hard.
b) ~~she would pay him back.~~
c) Fay would get promoted.
d) people would laugh.
e) she would be less stressed.
f) I wouldn't know what to say.

b) Are the sentences in **2a)** probably true (T) or probably false (F)?

1 [F] Erin owes Hal some money.

2 [ ] Don isn't going to ask her to marry him.

3 [ ] The speaker earns a lot of money.

4 [ ] Connor is going to dye his hair.

5 [ ] Debbie is going to leave.

6 [ ] Mo works hard.

3 Choose the correct words.

1 If we *had* / *would have* enough money, we *bought* / *would buy* a new computer.

2 I *would work* / *worked* harder if I *had* / *would have* more time.

3 If I *had* / *would have* a million pounds, I *gave* / *would give* half of it to charity.

4 How *did* / *would* you feel if I *would tell* / *told* everyone your secrets?

5 We *would have* / *had* to sell the house if I *lost* / *would lose* my job.

6 You *would learn* / *learned* a lot more if you *would speak* / *spoke* less and *listened* / *would listen* more.

7 I *would live* / *lived* in the north if it *wouldn't* / *didn't* rain so much.

8 If you *could* / *would be able to* hypnotise anyone in the world, who *did* / *would* you choose?

Edward Lenny Giles Alicia Ella Stan Susie and Cath

4 Stan is speaking about the people in his office. Look at the picture and write sentences with these words.

1 If / work more quickly, she / not have / to stay so late.

If Alicia worked more quickly, she wouldn't have to stay so late.

2 If / wear / a suit, I / promote / him to manager.

....

3 If / not talk / so much, they / do / a lot more work.

....

4 If / not go / out so late, he / not be / so tired.

....

5 If / be / more organised, she / not lose / everything.

....

6 If / live / nearer work, he / not arrive / late every day.

....

7 If I / not / worry so much, I / be / a lot happier!

....

5 Complete the sentences. Use the second conditional.

1 Vince never invites me to his parties, so I don't invite him to mine.

If Vince invited me to his parties, *I would invite him to mine.*

I would invite *Vince to my parties if he invited me to his.*

2 Chrissy doesn't enjoy going to the cinema because the seats aren't comfortable.

If the seats were comfortable, Chrissy ....

Chrissy would ....

3 We don't like children's books so we don't read Harry Potter.

If we ....

We would ....

4 My children don't live near me so I don't see them often.

If ....

I ....

12C Men of magic

Reading

 1 **Read the article quickly and choose the correct answer.**

What is the Balducci Levitation?
a) A trick you can do at home.
b) A trick only magicians can do.
c) A trick that needs special equipment.

Connecting words (2) V12.1

2 **Read the article again and choose the correct words/phrases.**

 3 **Are these sentences true (T) or false (F)?**

1 | F | David Blaine was the first person to do the Balducci Levitation.

2 | ☐ | Balducci was a magician from the USA.

3 | ☐ | The trick was invented by Edmund Balducci.

4 | ☐ | The trick doesn't involve a piece of wire.

5 | ☐ | You can do the trick in front of lots of people.

6 | ☐ | You need a pack of cards to do the trick.

7 | ☐ | You should wear trousers when you do the trick.

8 | ☐ | You need a mirror to do this trick.

 Reading and Writing Portfolio 12 p86

levitate (verb) to rise and float in the air without any physical support

THE BALDUCCI LEVITATION

The Balducci Levitation is a magic trick that David Blaine did on a TV show called *David Blaine: Street Magic*. He stood in front of a small group of people and then slowly, his feet started to lift off the ground. For a few seconds he was flying!

The trick is named after the American magician, Edmund Mariano Balducci (1907–1988). But Balducci didn't invent the trick and nobody knows who did. You might think that it's a piece of wire or perhaps a camera trick. In fact, it is much more simple than you think.

¹*First/Next* you need the right audience. Choose a small group of people who don't know you. ²*Then/When* do a few simple tricks, for example card tricks, and ³*next/when* your audience is ready and feeling magical, tell them you want to try a new trick. Then follow these simple instructions:

- ⁴*First/Next* ask the people to stand close together. ⁵*Next/When* stand about two to three metres away from the people. Turn to your side. ⁶*Finally/After that* the audience should only be able to see your feet on the ground. But in fact they can only see one of your feet.

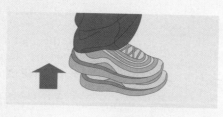

- ⁷*First/Then* slowly lift the foot that people can see. If you have a small audience, they won't be able to see your other foot because of your trousers and your shoe.

- ⁸*Finally/first*, when you are levitating at about 10 cm from the ground, stay there for one second. Then quickly fall back to the ground.

It sounds simple but, with practice, this trick can look amazing. Try it in front of the mirror. You'll be surprised!

Staying in touch

Reading a personal letter
Writing a letter to a friend
Review Present Simple; Past Simple

 Read the letter quickly and tick (✓) the topics Rich talks about.

a) his new job ✓
b) neighbours
c) his new colleagues
d) his new home
e) the journey to work
f) his children's new school
g) his next visit to England

 Read the letter again. Are these sentences true (T) or false (F)?

1 [T] Rich liked the people at his old company.

2 [ ] His commute to work is better now.

3 [ ] His computer is still in England at the moment.

4 [ ] He finds it difficult to talk to people in shops.

5 [ ] He speaks good German.

6 [ ] Rich and Mark both have children.

7 [ ] Rich wants Mark and his family to visit.

8 [ ] Rich is coming to England for a special dinner in October.

¹Chrummwisstrasse 47
8702 Kuesnacht
Zurich

²17ᵗʰ September

³Dear Mark,

⁴Thanks so much for your card.

⁵I really loved the party last week and I was quite sad at the end. I'm going to miss all the wonderful friends I made at the company. How are things without me?

I started work at my new place on Monday. The commute is a lot shorter. I catch a train near my house and I'm at work in fifteen minutes. It's amazing! I have time to play with Maggie before she goes to bed!

The house is nice – see the pictures. But we're really busy at the moment. A lot of things are still in boxes – including the computer – so I can't email at the moment.

We're enjoying learning a new language. The first time Maggie heard some children talking she cried. Then she said 'Daddy! What's wrong with them?' In fact, many of the Swiss speak English (and French and Italian!) so communicating in shops isn't difficult. Television is a bit harder! I watched the German 'Who Wants to Be a Millionaire?' the other night. I think I got two questions correct, but I don't know!

Victoria sends her love – she's cooking something Swiss at the moment. Remember: the flight is only 40 minutes! You, Tamsin and the children are always welcome.

⁶Anyway, that's about it for the moment. Look after yourself and keep in touch.

⁷All the best,

Rich

⁸PS I'm in London for a meeting at the end of October. Do you want to meet for dinner?

Help with Writing Informal letters

3 **a)** Look at the letter again. Match 1–8 to headings a)–h).

a) [3] greeting

b) [ ] the date

c) [ ] the main body of the letter

d) [ ] the beginning of the letter

e) [ ] the address

f) [ ] the closing sentences

g) [ ] adding extra information

h) [ ] the end of the letter

b) Notice these phrases in Rich's letter. Which are used at the beginning (B) and which at the end (E) of the letter?

a) [B] Thanks so much for …

b) [ ] How are things …

c) [ ] Victoria sends her love …

d) [ ] Anyway, that's about it for the moment.

e) [ ] Look after yourself and keep in touch.

f) [ ] All the best,

c) <u>Underline</u> the phrases in **3b)** in Rich's letter.

4 Look at Mark's reply to Rich's letter. Put the letter in the correct order.

A [ ]

Tamsin's out at yoga at the moment so it's a good time to write back. ¹She says hi to you and Victoria. The children are always on the computer so I can't email either.

²How is everything at the new place? What are your Swiss colleagues like? I can't believe your new commute. There was a strike here last week. On Thursday it took me over two hours to get to work. Are Swiss trains good?

The pictures are great. I showed them to everyone at work. It really isn't the same without you, Rich. I don't have anyone to talk to. And I'm doing too much work! It's great news that you're coming over. Do you know the date of your meeting? I'll try and find a traditional British restaurant for you. Fish and chips OK?

B [ ]

Monday 18th September

C [ ]

PS I will find some ticket prices, when I can use the computer …

D [ ]

Dear Rich,

E [ ]

³Best wishes,
Mark

F [1]

25 South Avenue,
London
W12 2HE

G [ ]

⁴Thank you for your letter.

H [ ]

⁵Anyway, that's all the news for you. ⁶Take care and write back soon.

5 Match phrases 1–6 in **bold** in Mark's letter to phrases a)–f) in **3b)**.

1 _c)_   3 ....   5 ....

2 ....   4 ....   6 ....

6 **a)** Imagine you have moved to another country. Make notes on your new home and your new routine.

where you now live	
your new work	
your new commute	
a new language	

b) Write an informal letter to a good friend about your new life.

- Use your notes from **6a)**.
- Use the organisation of an informal letter in **3a)**.
- Use the phrases in **3b)**.
- Read and check for mistakes.
- Give your letter to your teacher next class.

Tick the things you can do in English in the Reading and Writing Progress Portfolio, p88.

An email with news

Reading an email with news
Writing connecting words (1): addition and contrast; an email (1)
Review Past Simple for telling a story; relationships

 Read the email quickly and choose the correct answers.

1 The email is …
   a) to Poppy and from Katy.
   b) from Poppy and to Katy.

2 Poppy and Katy are probably …
   a) colleagues.
   b) friends.

3 Ollie is Katy's …
   a) boyfriend.
   b) husband.

Dear Poppy,

How are you? Sorry I didn't reply to any of your emails, but I only checked today. Last week was a busy and very exciting week.

Ollie and I went out for dinner on Friday. We were celebrating our anniversary – we started going out four years ago. Four years! I can't believe it. He wanted to surprise me and he did – we went to Fifteen – Jamie Oliver's new restaurant! The food was amazing. It's also cheaper than I thought. However, that's not the reason I'm writing …

After the meal, we were having coffee and Ollie asked for the bill. When it came, he gave it to me. I laughed, but then I saw a lot of waiters looking at me. What's more, they were all smiling. I didn't know what was happening. When I looked at the bill, I knew. It just said 'Will you marry me, Katy?' in Ollie's handwriting. Then Ollie gave me a small box. It was a ring! I put it on and very nervously said yes. The waiters started clapping and I went very red!

Someone in the restaurant gave us a bottle of champagne. We didn't drink it, though. We can have it when you next come to London. And we can also go shopping! I need a wedding dress and someone to help me choose it!

Love,

Katy

 Read the email again and answer the questions.

1 Why didn't Katy email Poppy last week?

   Because she only checked today.

2 Why did Katy go out for dinner with Ollie last week?

   ----

3 Who chose the restaurant?

   ----

4 Why did Ollie give Katy the bill?

   ----

5 What does Katy want to do with Poppy?

Help with Writing Connecting words(1): addition and contrast

3 **a)** Look at these sentences. Notice how we use *and*, *also* and *what's more* to give more information.

1 Last week was a busy **and** very exciting week.

2 Last week was a busy week. It was **also** exciting.

3 Last week was a busy week. **What's more**, it was very exciting.

b) Underline the examples of *also* and *what's more* in Katy's email.

4 **a)** Look at these sentences. Notice how we connect the ideas using *but*, *however* and *though*.

1 Sorry I didn't reply to any of your emails, **but** I only checked today.

2 Sorry I didn't reply to any of your emails. **However**, I only checked today.

3 Sorry I didn't reply to any of your emails. I only checked today, **though**.

b) Underline the examples of *however* and *though* in Katy's email.

5 Choose the correct answers in the rules.

- *And* links ideas in one sentence. *Also* and *What's more* link ideas in *one sentence*/⟨*two sentences*⟩.

- *But* contrasts ideas in one sentence. *However* and *though* contrast ideas in *one sentence/two sentences*.

- We put *also* *before/after* the verb *be* and *before/after* other verbs.

- We put *however* at the *beginning/end* of a sentence and *though* at the *beginning/end*.

TIP! • We always put a comma (,) after *What's more* and *However*.

6 Write these sentences again. Use the words/phrases in brackets.

1 I didn't invite him and I didn't want him to come. (What's more)
   I didn't invite him. What's more, I didn't want him to come.

2 She sent me a text, but I didn't reply. (though)
   ....

3 He owns the restaurant and he's a very good cook. (also)
   ....

4 I'm not married, but I've got a girlfriend. (However)
   ....

5 We bought a new car last year and Mike got a new job. (What's more)
   ....

6 I met a nice man last week, but he's already going out with someone. (However)
   ....

7 We got engaged last month, but we're not going to get married until next year. (though)
   ....

8 My parents met in 1975 and they got married that year. (also)
   ....

7 **a)** Imagine you have some exciting news about an event in your family. Look at these questions and make notes in boxes 1–4.

When is the event?	1
Who does it involve?	2
What happened?	3
What is going to happen next?	4

b) Write an email to a friend about your news.

- Use your notes from **7a)**.
- Use connecting words from **3a)** and **4a)** to connect your ideas.
- Read and check for mistakes.
- Give your email to your teacher next class.

Tick the things you can do in English in the Reading and Writing Progress Portfolio, p88.

Applying for a job

Reading a formal letter
Writing a curriculum vitae (CV)
Review personal details;
employment; looking for a job

 Read the advertisements and the letter. Answer the questions.

1 What are the advertisements for?

....

2 Who is the letter to?

....

3 Which job in the advertisements is she interested in?

....

4 Who is the letter from?

....

5 Why is he writing?

....

 Read the letter again and complete Ms Weston's notes.

A Website designer
Some experience needed.

B
Hotel Management
Training position in busy UK Hotel.
Languages needed.

C Secretary with languages
Computer skills needed.

D
ASSISTANT CHEF
Are you interested in a career in food?
No experience necessary.

Eats Restaurant

good things

Training is ¹ _on-the-job_ and at ² _college_ .

Sick ³ _____ and ⁴ _____ pay.

Good ⁵ _____ for ⁶ _____ after training.

bad things

Training is ⁷ _____ years.

Long working ⁸ _____ – at least nine a day!

Not much ⁹ _____ while training.

---

12 Cross Street
Liverpool
L12 4HR

Dear Ms Weston,

Thank you for your recent phone call about the position of assistant chef at Eats restaurant. I am writing to summarise* our conversation.

The job is for an assistant chef at our restaurant in Liverpool. No experience is necessary, but training takes two years. There is a lot of on-the-job training, but assistant chefs also take courses at the colleges in Liverpool, Manchester and London.

Staff work very hard at the restaurant. Assistant chefs usually work at least nine hours a day and sometimes for longer. The salary is low* while you are training, but we also offer holiday pay and sick pay. After training there are good opportunities for promotion.

If you are interested in the job, please send your CV to the above address. We will contact you to arrange an interview.

Yours sincerely,

Simon Parks

Simon Parks

Manager
Eats Restaurant

*summarise = describe the main facts   *low = not much

3 Read the CV and write the correct information in a)–f).

a) Her full name. _Lauren Elizabeth Weston_

b) Her email address. _____

c) The year she was born. _____

d) The name of her school. _____

e) A restaurant she worked at in France.

_____

f) A prize she won. _____

Lauren Elizabeth Weston

5 Circus Street
Liverpool. L22 5EG

laurenweston@mailme.net
Home: 0151 565732 Mobile: 07986 004121

Date of Birth: 5.11.1988
Nationality: British

1 ....

**2004–2005 Northampton College,
Hospitality and Catering course**
This course included work on:
• preparation of meat, vegetables
• food presentation
• menu preparation

1999–2004 Liverpool High School for Girls
8 GCSEs* including Mathematics, English and French.

2 ....

Summer 2002 Le Moulin, Chantonnay, France
Trainee chef experience including vegetable preparation.

Summer 2001 The Fox Public House, Speke
Bar work serving food and drinks to customers.

3 ....

2003 Winner of Liverpool Young Chef of the Year

4 ....

• Computers – word processing and spreadsheets
• Fluent speaker of French

REFEREE*

Mrs M. James
Hospitality and Catering Courses
Northampton College

---

*GCSE = General Certificate of Secondary Education, an English school exam
*referee = someone who can describe you when you are applying for a job

---

Help with Writing A curriculum vitae or CV

 4 **a)** Look at the organisation of the CV. Fill in gaps 1–4 in the CV with headings a)–d).

a) WORK EXPERIENCE
b) ADDITIONAL INFORMATION
c) ACTIVITIES AND INTERESTS
d) EDUCATION AND QUALIFICATIONS

b) Read the CV tips and complete the table with examples from Ms Weston's CV.

CV tips	example
Use **bold** for important words.	_Lauren Elizabeth Weston_
Use bullet points (•) for lists.	
Include important courses.	
Summarise your school examinations.	
Include important work experience.	
List other skills you have.	

5 **a)** Choose one of the job advertisements A–C in **1**. Make notes for your CV in the table. You can invent details if necessary.

courses and qualifications	
work experience	
include other skills you have	

b) Write your CV for one of the advertisements in **1**.

• Use your notes from **5a)**.
• Use the organisation of Ms Weston's CV.
• Use the CV tips in **4**.
• Read and check for mistakes.
• Give your guide to your teacher next class.

Tick the things you can do in English in the
Reading and Writing Progress Portfolio, p88.

A great film

1 Read about the Four Word Film Review website and match reviews a)–d) with four films from **1** on page 20.

> The Four Word Film Review (www.fwfr.com) is a website with film reviews. All the reviews are sent by readers of the website. And all the reviews are only four words.

Here are a some examples:

a) Station romance stays still. _Brief Encounter_

b) Prize: evening with star. ....

c) Future time, mystery crime. ....

d) Hitchcock's famous hotel horror. ....

2 Read the review about *The Ladykillers* quickly and choose the best four-word film review.

1 ☐ Old lady robs bank.

2 ☐ Nice musicians help woman.

3 ☐ Professor doesn't tell truth.

3 Read the review again and complete column A in the table.

	A	B
the year of the film		
the location of the film	London	
name of main characters		
name of main actor	Alec Guinness	
other films made by the main actor		
name of the director		
the story		
the music	no information	
name of the reviewer		

4 Another four-word film review of *The Ladykillers* is 'Old woman gets rich'. What do you think happens at the end?

....

....

Reading a film review
Writing describing a film
Review Present Simple for telling a story; Past Simple; Present Perfect for experiences; films

FILM REVIEW

The Ladykillers – a classic British film

I didn't think I'd like *The Ladykillers*. It's a British film, made in 1955, and I don't really like old films. But what a surprise! I haven't seen a better film this year.

The plot is simple. An old lady, Mrs Wilberforce, lives alone in a house in London. A man called Professor Marcus rents a room in Mrs Wilberforce's house. He says he is a classical musician, but in fact Marcus and his 'band' are bank robbers*.

The Professor and his friends get the money, but then Mrs Wilberforce finds out. She wants them to give it back so they decide to kill her. But this is more difficult than they think!

The acting is brilliant. Katie Johnson plays kind Mrs Wilberforce. And you should know Professor Marcus (Alec Guinness) from many films. Over 20 years later he was in Star Wars! The director is Alexander Mackendrick.

I watched *The Ladykillers* with my 14-year-old son. We both loved it. It is a classic film with classic actors and is suitable for the whole family.

There is also a 2004 remake* of the film with Tom Hanks. I will compare the two films soon.

★★★★★   Melissa Parks

*robber = someone who steals
*remake = make again

Help with Writing Describing a film; verb forms; film vocabulary

5 a) Which of these sentences talk about the story and which talk about the reviewer's reactions to the film? Write S (story) or R (reactions).

1 [S] An old lady, Mrs Wilberforce, lives alone in a house in London.

2 [ ] I haven't seen a better film this year.

3 [ ] In fact, Marcus and his 'band' are bank robbers.

4 [ ] We both loved it.

b) Answer the questions.

1 Which verb form does the reviewer use to talk about the story? ....

2 Which verb forms does the reviewer use to talk about her feelings and reactions to the film?

.... and ....

6 Notice how the reviewer uses the film vocabulary to describe *The Ladykillers*. Tick the topics which the reviewer talks about.

[ ] the acting   [ ] the music   [ ] the director   [ ] the place where the film happens

[ ] the photography   [ ] the story   [ ] the price   [ ] other films by the actor or director

7 Read Jen's letter to her friend, Sally. Fill in the gaps with the correct form of the verbs in brackets.

Dear Sally,

Do you remember we were talking about the actor Ewan McGregor? Well, Michael and I watched a film called 'Big Fish' and he was in it. It's the best film I ¹ 've seen (see) for a long time.

A man called Will Bloom ² .... (come) home when he ³ .... (hear) his father, Ed, is dying. Ed is famous in his town for telling stories about his amazing life. Will ⁴ .... (not believe) the stories, but he ⁵ .... (listen) to them one last time.

Ewan McGregor ⁶ .... (play) the young Ed. He rescues his town, fights in a war, works in a circus and, of course, ⁷ .... (meet) Will's mother. My favourite story ⁸ .... (be) when Ed ⁹ .... (become) a bank robber.

We really ¹⁰ .... (enjoy) the film, Sally. The music was excellent, too – a mix of rock 'n' roll and classical music. There ¹¹ .... (be) some great actors in it, including Jessica Lange and Danny DeVito. And yes, I ¹² .... (cry) at the end! Even Michael ¹³ .... (like) it.

Well that's enough from me. Next time you're in the video shop, look out for 'Big Fish'.

Love, Jen

PS The director is Tim Burton. He made 'Edward Scissorhands' – I think we watched it together.

8 Think about a film you have seen recently. Fill in column B in the table in **3**.

9 Write a letter to a friend. Tell him/her about a film you saw recently.

- Use your notes from **8**.
- Use the Present Simple to describe the story and the Past Simple or Present Perfect to describe your reactions to the film.
- Include the film vocabulary from **6**.
- Read and check for mistakes.
- Give your letter to your teacher next class.

Tick the things you can do in English in the Reading and Writing Progress Portfolio, p88.

Which language school?

Reading language school brochures
Writing formal and informal letters
Review requests; Present Simple

1 Read the brochures about the language courses in the UK. Then fill in the table. If there is no information, write DS (doesn't say).

school	town	name of course	lessons per week	hours per week	minimum age	maximum number of students
The Select School	¹Cambridge	2	DS	3	DS	4 (only 1 in 1-1 classes)
Fluency First College	5	Let's talk	6	7	8	DS
9	10	English Express	11	12	13	14

A

The Select School of English
Intensive English *Plus*

This course offers 15 hours of General English lessons and four hours of one-to-one classes* every week. The main course develops grammar, vocabulary and skills in a class of no more than 10 students. In the one-to-one classes you can plan your work with a teacher and work on areas that are important to your studies or work.
Cambridge is a beautiful city and home of one of the world's most famous universities. London is only 50 minutes by train.

B

Fluency First College

Fluency First College
***Let's Talk* – communication and special interests**
The focus of *Let's Talk* is on communicating clearly in everyday language. Every week there are 14 general language lessons and 8 special interest lessons. Subjects include: business language, culture and customs, language and the media and literature
   Let's Talk is available at our school in the historical city of Bath.

C

Language Links
Brighton is often called 'London by the Sea'. There are so many things to do! And London is only 55 minutes away on the train.
English Express
- The school offers four-week courses of 28 lessons per week (24 hours).
- There are 21 lessons of general English and 7 lessons that develop skills.
- The maximum class size is 12 and the minimum age of students is 17.

*one-to-one classes = classes with one student and one teacher

2 Paola, Emre, Daiki and Kiko are going to study English. Read about the kind of language school they would like. Choose a school (A–C) for each person.

I'm a student at a business college in Milan, Italy. I want to learn language that is important for my degree. It's not important where I go in England.

Paola

I learned English when I was at school and now I want to use it again. I think I'm Pre-intermediate level, but I need some extra help.

Emre

We want a course for about a month. We want to study together and we want to work really hard. We'd like to be near London because we like going out.

Daiki and Kiko

3 Read Paola's letter to a language school. Choose the correct phrases in 1–4.

> Via Della Colonella, 32
> Roma 00186
> Italy
> ¹ 12ᵗʰ March 2006
> Paola Conte

Fluency First College
32 Bristol Road
Bath
BA2 9HE

Dear ²*Sir/Madam,/Language Links,*

I am writing to you **with reference to** your advertisement for one-month courses in Bath.

I would be grateful if you could send me **further** information about the course including: the minimum age of students, the maximum number of students in a class and the length of the lessons. At the moment, I'm studying at a business college in Italy, so **I am interested in** the special interest lesson of 'Business language'. **Could you** send me some details on this course?

I would also like some information about accommodation. Do students stay at the school or with families?

Finally, **would you be able to** send me some brochures about the city of Bath?

I look forward to hearing from you soon.

Yours ³*sincerely/faithfully,*

Paola Conte

⁴*Paola Conte/12ᵗʰ March 2006*

Tick the things you can do in English in the Reading and Writing Progress Portfolio, p88.

Help with Writing Formal and informal letters

4 **a)** Complete the table with the words/phrases in the box.

> ~~Dear Sir/Madam,~~   ~~All the best,~~   Yours sincerely,   Love, Kiko
> Yours faithfully,   Dear John,   Dear Mrs Austin,

	formal letters	informal letters
starting a letter if you:		
know the person's name	1	2
don't know the person's name	³*Dear Sir/ Madam,*	
ending a letter if you:		
know the person's name	4	5
		or ⁶*All the best,*
don't know the person's name	7	

b) In formal letters we use formal phrases. Match the words/phrases in **bold** in the letter to informal meanings 1–7.

1 Can you: _Could you_ and ....

2 Please can you: ....

3 about: ....

4 I like the idea of: ....

5 I also want: ....

6 more: ....

7 Please write back soon: ....

....

5 **a)** Imagine you are writing a letter to a language school in the UK. Make notes in the table.

Who are you writing to?	
What is your language level?	
What information do you need?	
Do you have any special interests?	

b) Write a formal letter to a language school asking for information.

- Use your notes from **5a)**.
- Use the formal phrases in Paola's letter.
- Read and check for mistakes.
- Give your letter to your teacher next class.

Reading and Writing Portfolio 6

Writing notes

Reading notes and messages
Writing messages: missing words; common abbreviations
Review Present Simple; Past Simple; *be going to*; articles; auxiliaries

1 Read messages and notes A–F quickly. Which note is about:

1 someone's work? **D**

2 a social arrangement? ☐

3 a meal? ☐

4 a TV programme? ☐

5 money? ☐

6 a job application? ☐

2 Read the messages and notes again and answer the questions.

1 Who is going to do some sport? __Steve__

2 Who is having a drink? ....

3 Who wrote the message about Nick? ....

4 Who likes the TV programme *EastEnders*? ....

5 Who hasn't got any money? ....

6 Whose CV did Ruby read? ....

Help with Writing Notes

3 Look at the notes in **1** again. Notice how we often miss out pronouns, auxiliary verbs *be* and *have*, and articles.

- pronouns and auxiliary verbs:
  ~~I am~~ Going to play football.
  ~~I've~~ Read your CV.
- articles:
  Can't remember ~~the~~ name.
  Am at ~~the~~ café in Shirland Rd. with ~~a~~ couple of friends.

TIP! • We don't miss out *will* or *should* in notes: ✗ Will eat something at pub. not ~~Eat something at pub.~~

4 Write the full form of these sentences from the notes from **1**.

1 Nick rang. __He__ wants you to be in __the__ office early tomorrow.

2 Clare – __I've__ read your CV.

3 .... think it's good.

4 .... need to check spelling & punctuation, though!

5 .... can't understand .... video recorder.

6 .... back at about 11.

7 .... need to pay .... cleaner today.

8 .... haven't got anything!

A Am at café in Shirland **Rd.** with couple of friends. Can't remember name – Italian place. Come down!
Sam

B Clare – Read your CV. Think it's good. Need to check spelling **&** punctuation, though! Ruby

C Fiona,
Going to play football. Don't worry about dinner. Will eat something at pub.
Love you **v.** much.
Steve

D Nick rang. Wants you to be in office early tomorrow – before 8 if **poss.**
Tara

E Can't understand video recorder – can you record EastEnders for me? Please! It's on at 7.30.
PTO

Don't forget. Back about 11. Love Mum x

F Need to pay cleaner today. Haven't got anything! **Pls.** can you leave £20? **Thx!**
Lucy

These messages are too long. Write them again using the number of words in brackets or less.

1

To Dad,
I'm going to the gym. I will be back at six o'clock and I will be very hungry!
Tracy
(14 words)

~~Dad I'm going~~ Going to the gym. ~~I will be back~~ Back
at six o'clock ~~and I~~ will be very hungry! Tracy

2

Dear Mel,
This is very important: there is a message on the answerphone from the police. They found your car in Brook Road!
Adrian
(15 words)

Mel

3

Hi Sarah,
If possible, can you call the garage about the car? It should be ready today. Thanks.
From Chris
(15 words)

4

Dear Jack,
Your flatmate rang. Have you got her keys? She can't find them and she can't leave the house! Please ring her.
Best wishes,
Lyn
(20 words)

5

Hello Jan,
I'm going to the cinema in Mason Road to see the new Brad Pitt film.
Please turn over.
I'm meeting Rob for a drink first. Do you want to come?
Yours, Macy.
(25 words)

Help with Writing Notes and abbreviations

 Look at the abbreviations in **bold** in the notes in **1**. We often use abbreviations in notes and messages. Match abbreviations 1–7 to meanings a)–g).

1	Rd.	a)	and
2	&	b)	please turn over
3	v.	c)	very
4	poss.	d)	Thanks
5	PTO	e)	Please
6	Pls.	f)	possible
7	Thx	g)	Road

 Read the messages in **5** again and replace as many words as possible with the abbreviations in **6**.

1 *Going to gym. Back at six & will be v. hungry!*

2

3

4

5

8 **a)** Read these situations and answer the questions.

1 You can't find something important in your flat. Write a note to your flatmate and ask him/her if he/she knows where it is. Tell your flatmate to phone you if he/she can help and leave a phone number.

   a) What are you looking for?
   b) What is your phone number?

2 You are going to do some sport. Write a note to your flatmate and say where you are going and when you will be back. Say if you want dinner.

   a) Where are you going?
   b) When will you be back?
   c) Do you want dinner?

b) Write notes for the situations in **8a)**.
● Don't use pronouns, auxiliary verbs or articles.
● Use some abbreviations from **6**.
● Read and check for mistakes.
● Give your notes to your teacher next class.

Tick the things you can do in English in the Reading and Writing Progress Portfolio, p88.

Writing to complain

 1 Read the advertisements and fill in gaps 1–5 in the table.

	A	B
advert is for?	1	cultural holidays
where?	2	4
the staff?	3	qualified teachers
price includes?	breakfast	5

3 Read the letter quickly and answer the questions.

1 Who wrote the letter?

....

2 Which advertisement is the writer complaining about?

....

A ## Seaview, Brighton

Seaview is a 3-star hotel ^{a)}**in the centre of the town.** We have clean, spacious rooms with air conditioning, a balcony and ^{b)}**a sea view.**
^{c)}**Friendly and helpful staff.**
^{d)}**Breakfast included.**

Phone 01273 324530 for a reservation.

B ## Shakespeare Tours

Enjoy some cultural entertainment near ^{e)}**quiet** Stratford-Upon-Avon with *Shakespeare Tours.*
^{f)}**Qualified university teachers** give talks on Shakespeare.
^{g)}**Organised** trips to the ^{h)}**theatre.**
Prices include all talks and theatre tickets.

Call 01233 372831 for prices and booking.

12 Ford St.
London
W2 5GE

11 Lewis Rd.
Brighton
BR12 7NH

Dear Sir/Madam,

¹ I recently spent three days at your hotel and I was extremely unhappy with the hotel, my room and the service.

² ● The advertisement says that the hotel is in the centre of Brighton. It is at least 20 minutes from the centre of Brighton.

● The hotel is called Seaview and the advertisement says rooms have a sea view. However, my room was opposite a car park!

● The breakfast at the hotel was the worst I have ever had – a piece of toast and cup of tea.

³ I complained about the situation to your staff. They were rude and extremely unhelpful. I tried to speak to the manager, but he was not available.

⁴ I would like a refund* for at least one of the nights I spent at Seaview. For a three-star hotel, the room, service and facilities were very poor.

I look forward to your explanation of the complaints in my letter.

Yours faithfully,

M. Griffin

Martin Griffin

 2 Match complaints 1–8 to phrases a)–h) in **bold** in the advertisements.

1 [a] It was 20 minutes from Brighton.

2 [ ] Our room was opposite a car park.

3 [ ] They were university students!

4 [ ] There was only one Shakespeare play.

5 [ ] Toast and a cup of tea.

6 [e] Quiet? It was opposite the bus station!

7 [ ] They were rude and extremely unhelpful.

8 [ ] But they were completely disorganised – just like the staff!

*refund = money returned to you because you are not happy with something you bought

Help with Writing Organising a letter of complaint; useful phrases

4 **a)** The letter in **3** is organised into four main paragraphs. Match descriptions a)–d) to paragraphs 1–4.

a) ☐ The details of his complaint. c) ☐ Why he is writing.

b) ☐ What he tried to do. d) ☐ What he would like the company to do.

b) Notice how the letter has separate bullet points (•) for each complaint.

5 **a)** Fill in the gaps in useful phrases a)–e) with these words.

advertisement about explanation extremely would

a) The _advertisement_ says …

b) I was _____ unhappy with …

c) I complained _____ the situation …

d) I look forward to your _____ of …

e) I _____ like a refund …

b) Look at the letter in **3** again and check your answers to **5a)**. Then <u>underline</u> phrases a)–e) in the letter. Notice how the sentences continue.

6 **a)** Look at Corinne Blake's letter of complaint to *Shakespeare Tours*. Write (X) where she should start a paragraph and (•) where she should put a bullet point.

Dear Sir/Madam,
X I recently had a week's holiday with *Shakespeare Tours* in Stratford. I'm writing because I was ¹**very, very unhappy** with my holiday. ²**It says** that Stratford-upon-Avon is quiet. But our accommodation was opposite the bus station. The advertisement says that the teachers are qualified. They were university students. We went to the theatre three times. Only one of the plays was Shakespeare. ³**I said some things** about the situation to the staff on the course, but they were as disorganised as the trips to the theatre! I would like ⁴**the money back** for part of the holiday. My week with *Shakespeare Tours* was the worst experience I've ever had. ⁵**Please write to me soon**.
Yours faithfully,
Corinne Blake

b) Match phrases 1–5 in the letter to phrases a)–e) in **5a)**.

1 _b)_   3 _____   5 _____

2 _____   4 _____

7 **a)** Look at the advertisement and questions 1–4. Then complete the table with your complaints.

1 Was it 40 minutes from London?

2 Were they experienced and qualified?

UNIVERSITY STUDY TOURS
Study English in Oxford, only **40 minutes from London**.
- **Experienced and qualified teachers.**
- A maximum class size of **12 students.**
- **Excellent accommodation** with local families.

UST

3 How many students were there in the class?

4 What was the accommodation like?

point	complaint
1	Oxford is at least 55 minutes from London by train.
2	
3	
4	

b) Write a letter of complaint to *University Study Tours*.

- Use your notes from **7a)**.
- Organise your letter into paragraphs.
- Use phrases from **5a)** in your letter.
- Read and check for mistakes.
- Give your letter to your teacher next class.

Tick the things you can do in English in the Reading and Writing Progress Portfolio, p88.

A guide to studying abroad

Reading a magazine article
Writing connecting words (2): similarities, differences and comparisons; a description
Review comparatives; verb patterns

 1 Read the article quickly and match headings a)–e) to paragraphs 1–5.

a) Holidays
b) Living costs
c) Time and temperature
d) ~~People~~
e) Food

 2 Read the article again. Are these sentences true (T) or false (F)?

The article says ...

1 [F] films and TV are a good way to learn about American culture.

2 [ ] many Americans like shouting at sporting events.

3 [ ] meals in restaurants are usually bigger in the USA than the UK.

4 [ ] leaving a tip in bars is not usually necessary.

5 [ ] there are fewer national holidays in the USA than in most other countries.

6 [ ] in general the cost of living is higher in the USA than in the UK.

7 [ ] the difference between the time in New York and San Francisco is three hours.

8 [ ] in winter, the north is hotter than the south.

NYC College:
Advice for students studying in the USA

Everyone knows something about the USA and the Americans. But films and television often give the wrong idea about this country and its people.

¹ People

The popular stereotype* of Americans is that they are rude and shout a lot – especially at sports events! In comparison with the British, Americans are more informal. For example, they often call teachers by their first names. However, many Americans are like people in other countries – polite and helpful, especially with foreigners.

2 _____

The size of meals in American restaurants is very large, especially compared to the UK. And if you can't finish your meal, it's common to ask to take some home with you. This is completely different from the UK! And don't forget to leave a tip* in restaurants and bars. This is very important – you should leave about 15% of the bill.

3 _____

Americans don't get much holiday. Most people have about two weeks of holiday each year. This is quite unlike other western countries. The average is about four weeks holiday. However, Americans also have about ten national holidays each year. This is similar to most countries.

4 _____

Compared with the UK, the USA is generally a lot cheaper for clothes, eating out, entertainment and much more! But the cost of renting a flat is similar to the UK and is quite expensive in big cities.

5 _____

The USA is an enormous country and there are four different time zones in the USA. So when it's 10 a.m. in New York, it's 7 a.m. in San Francisco. Don't forget this when you're phoning someone! In comparison with the north, winters in the south are not usually very cold. Check the weather in the area you are going to.

*stereotype = an idea about what people or things are like that is wrong
*a tip = money you give a waiter/waitress to thank them for the service

Help with Writing Connecting words (2): comparisons, similarities and differences

3 **a)** Look at these sentences from the article in **1**. Which phrases do we use to compare (C), to talk about similarities (S) and to talk about differences (D)?

1 ☐C☐ **Compared with** the UK, the USA is a lot cheaper.

2 ☐ ☐ Many Americans **are like** people in other countries.

3 ☐ ☐ This **is quite unlike** other western countries.

4 ☐ ☐ The size of meals in American restaurants is very large – especially **compared to** the UK.

5 ☐ ☐ **In comparison with** the north, winters in the south are not cold.

6 ☐ ☐ This is **completely different** from the UK.

7 ☐ ☐ The cost of renting a flat **is similar to** the UK.

b) Underline the sentences with the phrases in **3a)** in the article.

4 Fill in the gaps with these prepositions.

~~with~~	to	in	to
from	to	with	from

1 Compared *with* my road, yours is much quieter.

2 _____ comparison _____ other countries, the cost of living is much higher.

3 The weather is similar _____ my country.

4 Chinese food is completely different _____ Japanese food.

5 Our new house is very spacious compared _____ our old flat.

6 Which country do you think this is most similar _____ ?

7 Americans are not very different _____ other people.

5 Write these sentences again using the words in brackets and the phrases in **3a)**.

1 Jenny's personality is like her sister's.

   Jenny's personality is similar to her sister's. (similar)

2 Spanish food is very different from French food.

   _____ (unlike)

3 The weather here is similar to the weather at home.

   _____

   _____ (like)

4 The food is quite unlike anything I've ever tasted.

   _____

   _____ (different)

5 Houses in the UK are usually much smaller than houses in the USA.

   _____

   _____ (compared)

6 Italians usually dress better than British people.

   _____

   _____ (comparison)

7 His new film is almost the same as his last one.

   _____

   _____ (similar)

6 **a)** Make notes about your country on these topics.

people and stereotypes	
food	
holidays	
living costs	
time and temperature	

b) Write a guide to studying in your country.

● Use your notes from **6a)**.

● Organise your guide into different paragraphs with the headings in the table.

● Read and check for mistakes.

● Give your guide to your teacher next class.

Tick the things you can do in English in the Reading and Writing Progress Portfolio, p88.

Reading and Writing Portfolio 9

How are you?

Reading a personal email
Writing paragraphs; expressing sympathy and giving advice; an email (2)
Review giving advice; adjectives to describe feelings

1 Read the email quickly and find the names of:

a) Sara's ex-flatmate. ....

b) Sara's new flatmate. ....

c) Her flatmate's new boyfriend. ....

d) Dave's new boss. ....

2 Put events a)–f) in the correct order.

a) ☐ Hilary moved in.

b) ☐ Sara got a promotion at work.

c) ☐ 1 ☐ Sara's ex-flatmate bought a house.

d) ☐ Sara found Dave at her flat watching TV.

e) ☐ Suzy moved out of the flat.

f) ☐ Hilary started going out with Dave.

Help with Writing Paragraphs

3 **a)** Look at Sara's email again. How many paragraphs are there? ....

b) Match a)–e) to paragraphs 1–5 of the email.

a) ☐ 2 ☐ the background to Sara's problem

b) ☐ some good news

c) ☐ a request

d) ☐ Sara's main problem

e) ☐ greeting and introduction

QuickMAIL   SIGN OU

to: <geri.m@quickmail.com>; <matthew_976@quickmail.com>   addresse

subject: flatmate!!!   save dra

        send

Hi Geri and Matt,

[1]How are you? I'm so sorry I missed your birthday party on Saturday, Geri. I've got too much work at the moment and I had to go into the office at the weekend. Did you get my present? Was the party good?

[2]Actually I need some advice. My flatmate, Suzy, bought a house a couple of months ago so she moved out. I advertised the room and a colleague from work, Hilary, moved in. Everything was fine for the first month – we got on really well. Then a few weeks ago she started going out with another person from work – a man called Dave.

[3]The problem is that now he's spending a lot of his free time at our house. At the weekends he's here all the time! A few days ago I came home early because I wasn't feeling well. And guess who was sitting on my sofa, watching TV … yes, him! He had the day off and he must have a key! I was very annoyed, but I didn't say anything.

[4]Then, yesterday I got a promotion. I was really excited, but then I found out that I'm going to be Dave's boss! This is going to make the situation worse!

[5]Have you got any advice? You are both always good at these kinds of things.

Love,

Sara

4 Read Matt's reply to Sara's email. Put paragraphs A–D in the correct order.

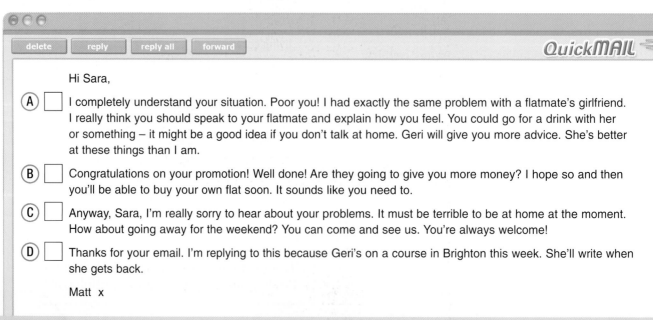

Hi Sara,

A ☐ I completely understand your situation. Poor you! I had exactly the same problem with a flatmate's girlfriend. I really think you should speak to your flatmate and explain how you feel. You could go for a drink with her or something – it might be a good idea if you don't talk at home. Geri will give you more advice. She's better at these things than I am.

B ☐ Congratulations on your promotion! Well done! Are they going to give you more money? I hope so and then you'll be able to buy your own flat soon. It sounds like you need to.

C ☐ Anyway, Sara, I'm really sorry to hear about your problems. It must be terrible to be at home at the moment. How about going away for the weekend? You can come and see us. You're always welcome!

D ☐ Thanks for your email. I'm replying to this because Geri's on a course in Brighton this week. She'll write when she gets back.

Matt x

5 **a)** Look at these useful phrases. Which are used for expressing sympathy (S) and which are used for giving advice (A)?

1 | S | Poor you!
2 | A | I really think you should …
3 | | How about … ?
4 | | You could …
5 | | I'm sorry to hear …
6 | | I completely understand …
7 | | It might be a good idea if …
8 | | It must be terrible …

b) Look at phrases 2–8 in **5a)** again. What usually comes after each phrase?

infinitive	infinitive with *to*
noun	*about* + noun
you	verb+*ing*

c) <u>Underline</u> the phrases in **5a)** in Matt's email to check.

6 **a)** Write these sentences of advice again using the words in brackets and the phrases in **5a)**.

1 Talk to your parents.

You could talk to your parents. (could)

2 Get another job.

....
.... (think)

3 You should save some money.

....
.... (idea)

4 Why don't you speak to your boss?

....
.... (how about)

5 What about asking for a week off work?

....
.... (could)

b) Write sentences expressing sympathy about these situations using the words in brackets and the phrases in **5a)**.

1 Jason lost his job last week.

I'm sorry to hear about Jason's job. (hear)

2 I lost my passport on holiday.

....
.... (terrible)

3 I've got money problems at the moment.

....
.... (understand)

4 My brother isn't well at the moment.

....
.... (hear)

7 **a)** Imagine you are Geri and you are replying to Sara's email. Make notes on your advice for each of Sara's problems.

Sara's problems	your advice
Dave spends too much time at her house.	
Hilary gave Dave a key to the house.	
Sara is now Dave's boss.	
Sara has too much work.	

b) Write your email to Sara.

- Use your notes from **7a)**.
- Organise your email into paragraphs.
- Use phrases from **5a)** for expressing sympathy and giving advice.
- Read and check for mistakes.
- Give your email to your teacher next class.

Tick the things you can do in English in the Reading and Writing Progress Portfolio, p88.

Giving an opinion

a) Read the short article from a newspaper. What is it asking?

....

Reading a letter to a newspaper
Writing connecting words (3); giving your opinion
Review connecting words; *used to*; agreeing and disagreeing

In Britain, about 12 million people bought something on the Internet during the last year. And experts predict that next year over 20 million of us will buy something online. Do you buy things on the Internet? Or do you prefer to go shopping in shops? Email us at opinions@dailynews.net. We'll print the best emails next week.

b) Are these sentences *for* (positive about) or *against* (negative about) shopping on the Internet? Write F (*for*) or A (*against*).

1 | A | You have to be at home when things arrive.

2 | | Things cost less on the Internet.

3 | | It's easier to find information about things on the Internet.

4 | | It isn't always safe to use your credit card on the Internet.

5 | | You can't see things clearly on the Internet.

6 | | You don't have to go out.

7 | | You can choose from more things on the Internet.

8 | | It's more enjoyable to go to the shops.

Read the email. Is the writer *for* or *against* shopping on the Internet? ....

a) Which three reasons in **1b)** does Harry talk about in his email in **2**?

.... , ... , ...

b) Can you think of any more reasons *for* or *against* shopping on the Internet?

for
_____
It's quicker than going to the shops.

against
_____
It's difficult to send things back.

---

[1]I used to buy almost everything on the Internet. I bought everything from CDs and DVDs to food from supermarkets. **But** I've had too many bad experiences and now I prefer to go to the shops.

[2]Firstly, things used to arrive when I was out. **Therefore**, I had to telephone the company and arrange for them to deliver things again. This was a waste of time and often I had to wait at home all day for something to arrive.

[3]My second point is that I often used to get the wrong things. **For example**, when I ordered food, there were often things missing or I received a 'similar' product.

[4]Finally, shopping on the Internet isn't as fun as going to the shops. **For instance**, you only see a picture of things **so** you can't see the quality of things you buy.

[5]**In my opinion** the Internet is fantastic for many things. **However, I personally believe** shopping is best done in shops!

Harry Johnson

Help with Writing
Beginning paragraphs; connecting words (3)

 4 a) Notice how Harry organises his email. Match a)–c) to paragraphs 1–5.

a) General statement about his experience and opinion: _1_

b) Arguments against shopping on the Internet: ......, ... and ......

c) Conclusion and his opinion: ......

b) <u>Underline</u> the words/ phrases that Harry uses to begin paragraphs 2–5.

c) Write the words/phrases in the table.

paragraph	word/phrase
2	
3	
4	
5	

 5 Look at the connecting words in **bold** in Harry's email. Put them in the correct place in the table.

giving examples	¹for example
	2
results	³so
	4
contrast	⁵but
	6
giving opinion	⁷in my opinion
	8

 6 a) Read Liz's email. Is she *for* or *against* shopping on the Internet?

---

subject: Shopping online   send

I only started using the Internet a year ago and I was a bit worried about buying things and sending my credit card details. ¹*However*/*Therefore*, a year later and I can't believe I used to go to the shops!

There are so many reasons why I love shopping on the Internet. ²*So*/*My first point is*, it's a lot a cheaper! ³*In my opinion*/*For instance*, a CD in the shop is about £13, but on the Internet I pay about £8.

⁴*I personally believe*/*Secondly*, things are delivered to my house and ⁵*for example*/ *therefore* I don't have to go out to the shops. It saves so much time!

⁶*Finally*/*However*, I don't have to listen to a sales person in a shop. They always think they know everything, ⁷*therefore*/*but* they never tell you anything useful!

⁸*I personally believe*/*Finally* there isn't an easier way to go shopping. I only go to shops for milk and bread. Perfect!

Liz Wharton

b) Read the email again and choose the correct words/phrases.

 7 a) Imagine your local newspaper is asking for opinions on different topics. Choose <u>one</u> of these topics. Write reasons *for* and *against* the topic.

1 Big shopping centres are better than streets of shops.
2 Everyone should have a credit card.
3 Children should save some of their pocket money every week.
4 Children should have lessons about spending and saving money at school.

for	against

b) Write an email *for* <u>or</u> *against* one of the topics.

- Use your notes from **7a)**.
- Use different paragraphs for each reason in **7a)**.
- Use words/phrases from **4b)** to begin each paragraph.
- Use words/phrases from **5** to connect sentences in your email.
- Read and check for mistakes.
- Give your emails to your teacher next class.

....

Tick the things you can do in English in the Reading and Writing Progress Portfolio, p88.

....

Telling a story

Reading a story
Writing verb forms in narratives; getting ideas; a narrative
Review Past Simple; Past Continuous; crime

 1 Read the story and put pictures A–F in the correct order 1–6.

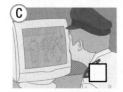

Operation Magician: The Robbery of the Century

It was a warm day in the middle of summer when Detective Inspector Sam Carr's phone rang. The man on the phone was speaking quietly, but Carr recognised his voice.

"There is going to be a robbery near the River Thames," the man said quietly. "The thieves are going to use a boat to escape."

Detective Inspector Carr rang his boss immediately.

"I've just heard something interesting," he said. And he explained the strange phone call to his boss.

The police immediately started an investigation*. They called it 'Operation Magician'. For the next few weeks they watched many different places near the River Thames including banks and also, of course, the huge Millennium Dome.

A few weeks later, Carr knew that the Dome was connected with the robbery. He also knew the names of the suspects. But what were the thieves planning? The police put cameras inside the Dome and started filming all the visitors.

On 1st September, 2000, three of the suspects were seen in the Dome. They were looking at the diamond exhibition in the Money Zone and they were especially interested in the Millennium diamonds – a collection worth over £200 million.

For the next month, Carr and his officers watched six suspects carefully. The men were testing a JCB digger* and a boat. But Carr still didn't know the time of the robbery. On 6th November Carr decided to change the real diamonds for fake* ones.

At 3.00 a.m. on 7th November, Carr arrived at the Dome and spoke to the 200 police officers who were waiting inside.

Six hours later the Dome was open. It was unusually busy for that time in the morning – Carr and his officers weren't wearing uniforms. They were dressed as tourists, cleaners and other workers.

*investigation = when the police try to discover the facts about a crime
*fake = not real   * JCB digger = a large machine used to move earth

2 Read the story again. Are these sentences true (T) or false (F)?

1 [T] Detective Inspector Carr knew the man on the phone.

2 [ ] Carr didn't tell anyone about the phone call.

3 [ ] The police immediately knew who the robbers were.

4 [ ] The thieves were planning to steal some diamonds and £200 million.

5 [ ] There were three men involved in the robbery.

6 [ ] The real diamonds were not in the Dome the time of the robbery.

Help with Writing
Verb forms in narratives

3 **a)** Match these verb forms to sentences a)–c) from the story.

1 Past Simple ....

2 Past Continuous ......

3 Past Simple passive ....

a) But what were the thieves planning?

b) On 1st September, 2000, three of the suspects were seen in the Dome.

c) The police immediately started an investigation.

b) Read the story again. Which are the two most common verb forms in the story?

....

and ....

c) Underline three examples of the most common verb forms in the story.

4 Read the end of the story. Fill in the gaps with the correct form of the verbs in brackets.

A few minutes after 9.30 a.m., while Carr and his officers ¹ _were walking_ (walk) around the Money Zone, a JCB digger ² _____ (crash) into the side of the Dome. Three men jumped out* of the digger and ³ _____ (break into) the glass case* with the worthless* diamonds.

Carr and his officers moved quickly. They took their guns out of the bags that they ⁴ _____ (carry) and ⁵ _____ (arrest) the men in the Money Zone. Outside another man ⁶ _____ (wait) in the boat. The police quickly arrested him. Operation Magician was a complete success. No one ⁷ _____ (shoot) or seriously hurt. Carr and his officers ⁸ _____ (be) amazed and very pleased.

After the robbery police ⁹ _____ (find) the receipt for the boat. What ¹⁰ _____ (be) the name on the receipt? Mr Diamond, of course.

*jump out = get out of a car, lorry, etc. suddenly and quickly
*(glass) case = furniture used for displaying something, for example, in a museum
*worthless = worth nothing

Help with Writing Getting ideas

5 **a)** Read the first sentence of the story. Can you remember the answers to questions 1–3?

It was a warm day in the middle of summer when Detective Inspector Sam Carr's phone rang.

1 Who was on the phone? _____

2 What did he tell Carr? _____

3 What did Carr do next? _____

b) Read the beginning of the story in 1 to check your answers.

c) You can get ideas about writing a story by thinking of questions about the first line. Look at this first line and notice the questions we can ask to get ideas.

First line of the story: As soon as Ashley walked into the room, she knew something was wrong.
Some questions: What was wrong? What could she see? What did Ashley do next?

TIP! • The first sentence of a story is important because it must interest the reader.

6 Match the first lines of stories 1–3 to questions a)–c).

1 ☐ Ian first met Nicole at a police station in central London.

2 ☐ Suzie recognised the writing on the letter immediately and suddenly felt very nervous.

3 ☐ Laurie had a problem, but he knew who to speak to.

a) Who wrote the letter? Why did she feel that way?

b) Why was he there? Why was she there?

c) What was his problem? Who was he going to talk to?

7 **a)** Choose <u>one</u> of the stories in **6**. Write another question. Then answer the three questions to get ideas for the story.

_____
_____
_____
_____
_____
_____
_____
_____
_____
_____
_____

b) Write a story beginning with one of the first lines in **6**.

• Use your notes from **7a)**.
• Use the Past Simple and Past Continuous in the story.
• Write about 100–150 words.
• Read and check for mistakes.
• Give your story to your teacher next class.

Tick the things you can do in English in the Reading and Writing Progress Portfolio, p88.

Reading and Writing Portfolio 12

What do you think?

Reading an online diary; a posting on a website
Writing common mistakes; describing your goals in a posting
Review Present Simple; Past Simple; Present Perfect; *be going to*

 Read the postings on the website quickly. Who has a problem with:

a) too much work? ....

b) a bad habit? ....

c) doing things too late? ....

X ← → 🖼 ⬜ | www.myblog/paulsmart.net

Exams, revision and my goals ...

I've just finished my exams. I don't know if I've passed yet, but I know that I was extremely nervous. I don't like exams and I probably never will. But if I fail these exams, I'll have to wait a whole year before I go to university.

So I started to think about my goals for the future. Next year, I'm going to be a lot more organised. I've already started – I tidied my room! I only started my revision a few weeks before my exams and I didn't have enough time. At university, I'm going to do some revision every month.

Have you made any decisions about things you're going to do differently? What are your goals for the next few months or year? Please write a comment on the website!

WRITTEN BY PAUL SMART AT 7.32 P.M.

VIEW MY PROFILE

MAKE A POSTING

PREVIOUS POSTINGS

Helen said ...

Hi Paul,

I don't have to do exams anymore, but I used to hate them!

I've made a few decisions recently. I smoke too much and I must give up soon. A few weeks ago a friend of mine went to see a hypnotist about smoking. She hasn't had a cigarette since then! She's says that she feels much better and much healthier. I'm going to try the same thing.

Secondly, I'm going to get fit. I don't do any exercise at the moment. I'm not fat, but I know I should do some. I went jogging a few days ago and it was really good. But my legs hurt a bit the next morning!

8.54 A.M.

Rupert said ...

Good luck with your goal, Paul!

My goal for the next year is a little strange. I'm going to work less! I'm divorced so I only see my children at the weekend. However, at the moment I can't always see them because I have so much work. They're growing up so fast and I feel really guilty. Your family should always be more important than work. So, I've decided not to work at weekends. I'm going to plan more days out with my children and I'm going to get to know them better.

2.12 A.M.

 Read the postings again and fill in gaps 1–7 in the table.

name	goal	what he/she has done so far	what he/she is going to do
Paul	¹*He's going to be more organised about exams.*	²	³
Helen	⁴	She went jogging.	⁵
Rupert	⁶	⁷	He's going to get to know his children better.
Alexandra	⁸	⁹	¹⁰
Marco	¹¹	¹²	¹³

Help with Writing Common mistakes

 3 a) Students often make these mistakes when they write.

1 *they're/there*: **They're** good friends. not ~~There good friends~~.

2 *too/to*: It's **too** hot. not ~~It's to hot~~.

3 *enough + noun*: I don't have **enough time**. not ~~I don't have time enough~~.

4 *comparative + than*: He's **older than** me. not ~~He's older that me~~.

b) Match types of mistakes 1–8 to examples a)–h).

1 irregular comparatives

2 auxiliary verbs

3 Present Simple *-s* with he/she/it

4 Present Continuous with state verbs (*like, hate,* etc.)

5 Past Simple

6 Present Perfect

7 *will, should, might*

8 conditionals

a) *Last week I went to the cinema.* not ~~Last week I've been to the cinema~~.

b) *This is better.* not ~~This is more good~~.

c) *If I see him, I'll tell him.* not ~~If I will see him, I will tell him~~.

d) *I haven't done it yet.* not ~~I didn't do it yet~~.

e) *She lives near me.* not ~~She live near me~~.

f) *You should stay in bed.* not ~~You should to stay in bed~~.

g) *I like my job.* not ~~I'm liking my job~~.

h) *I'm going to work harder.* not ~~I going to work harder~~.

 4 Read these postings on the website from Alexandra and Marco. Then fill in gaps 8–13 in the table in **2**.

Alexandra said …

I'm a student to so I know how you feel!

My goals are all about money. I always spend more money that I earn. What's more, I waste a lot of money on things I don't need. Last year I borrowed a lot of money from my parents. There very kind, but now I'm paying it back. Then if I will have enough money, I'll start saving. I also going to plan my spending. Can anyone recommend any good websites about money? I didn't find any yet.

8.05 A.M.

Marco said …

I found this website while I was looking for some advice on my situation. One of my goals for the next six months is to find a new job. I'm not hating the job I have at the moment. But I need to find something with more good opportunities for promotion. I've spoken to my boss about it and she understand the way I feel.

A couple of weeks ago I've sent out my CV to a few companies, but I haven't had any replies yet.

I think I must to stay in my job until I find another one. I haven't got money enough and unemployment benefit isn't much!

12.30 P.M.

 5 Read Alexandra's and Marco's postings again. Find 12 mistakes from **3a)** and **3b)** and correct them.

6 a) Think about some goals you have for the next few months or years. Make notes on these things.

- Your goal(s) _____

  _____

  _____

- What you have done so far _____

  _____

  _____

- What you are going to do _____

  _____

  _____

b) Write a posting for Paul's website about your goals.

- Use your notes from **6a)**.
- Read and check for the mistakes in **3a)** and **3b)**.
- Write your posting again if you want to.
- Give your posting to your teacher next class.

> Tick the things you can do in English in the Reading and Writing Progress Portfolio, p88.

Pre-intermediate Reading and Writing Progress Portfolio

Tick the things you can do in English.

Portfolio	Reading	Writing
1 p64	☐ I can understand a simple personal letter talking or asking about everyday life. ☐ I can understand descriptions of events.	☐ I can organise an informal letter (address, date, etc.). ☐ I can write a short personal letter describing experiences and events.
2 p66	☐ I can understand short narratives about everyday things. ☐ I can understand descriptions of events and feelings.	☐ I can use connecting words of addition and contrast. ☐ I can write an email to a friend. ☐ I can write a description of an event – real or imagined.
3 p68	☐ I can understand standard letters (for example from a business). ☐ I can find the most important information in advertisements in newspapers.	☐ I can write my CV in summary form.
4 p70	☐ I can understand the plot of a simple story. ☐ I can understand what is significant about the most important events.	☐ I can describe the plot of a film in a personal letter.
5 p72	☐ I can understand the most important information in simple brochures about language schools.	☐ I can reply in written form to advertisements and ask for more information about products. ☐ I can write a simple formal letter.
6 p74	☐ I can understand simple messages and notes from friends or colleagues.	☐ I can use abbreviations in notes and messages. ☐ I can write short simple notes and messages.
7 p76	☐ I can find the most important information in advertisements for holidays. ☐ I can understand complaints in a formal letter.	☐ I can use paragraphs in a letter. ☐ I can write a formal letter about my experiences on holiday. ☐ I can explain problems and ask for solutions.
8 p78	☐ I can understand the main points in a newspaper article.	☐ I can describe similarities and differences using phrases like *compared with*, *is quite unlike*, etc. ☐ I can write a simple guide about my country and can express personal views and opinions.
9 p80	☐ I can understand events, feelings and wishes in a private email.	☐ I can use paragraphs in an email. ☐ I can offer sympathy and give advice. ☐ I can write emails to friends.
10 p82	☐ I can understand facts in an email.	☐ I can use connecting words/phrases like *for instance, therefore, however* and *I personally believe*. ☐ I can use phrases to begin paragraphs. ☐ I can write a simple article on a topic I am interested in and give my personal opinion.
11 p84	☐ I can understand the plot of a story.	☐ I can write a clearly structured story.
12 p86	☐ I can find the most important information in a website posting.	☐ I can write a posting for a website giving factual information about my goals for the future.